SALES
LETTERS
THAT
SELL

SALES LETTERS THAT SELL

Laura Brill

AMACOM

American Management Association

New York · Atlanta · Boston · Chicago · Kansas City · San Francisco · Washington, D.C.
Brussels · Mexico City · Tokyo · Toronto

Library of Congress Cataloging-in-Publication Data

Brill, Laura.
     Sales letters that sell / Laura Brill.
       p. cm.
    Includes index.
    ISBN 0-8144-7945-6 (paper)
    1. Sales letters. I. Title.
    HF5730.B75   1997
    658.8'1—dc21   97-2279
                                 CIP

Printing number

10 9 8 7 6 5 4 3 2

For **Paul,** my muse
 Matt, my mentor
 Rick . . . my man for all seasons

Table of Contents

SALES LETTERS THAT SELL

Introduction

One central principle should govern your writing today: If a technique makes your letter successful, use it. Otherwise, try a different approach.

As times change, so do both our readers and the rules. When I taught English, it all seemed so simple. There was a body of knowledge considered to be gospel. Much of it was derived from Latin, which we all know is a dead language.

In the twenty years I have been teaching business communications, I have seen a huge change in what is acceptable—mostly based on a pragmatic approach. We have begun to use language that is more conversational and reader-friendly because we know it works for today's readers.

Here are some concepts that are considered correct today that may well surprise you.

1. **You may end a sentence with a preposition, especially if it makes the sentence read better.**

   compare:

   Here are the brochures for which you have been waiting.

   * * * * *

   Here are the brochures you have been waiting for.

2. **You may begin sentences with *and, but, because, although, or I.*** Professional writers use *and* and *but* to open sentences or

even paragraphs because these words create a conversational flow.

3. **Today's grammar books suggest using a comma before the *and* in a series.**

> I bought apples, bananas, and oranges.

Since most people are not aware that this rule has changed, it's not a major problem if you ignore it.

4. **Contractions (*you'll, we're*) are not only acceptable for sales letters, they are desirable.** They personalize your writing and make you sound friendly.

Sometimes even when you're correct, you're perceived as being incorrect. Here are some examples of confusion in our language today.

1. ***Data* is now acceptable as being either singular or plural.** But if you say *The data is inconclusive*, your reader may think you're incorrect.
2. **The dictionary has accepted the alternative spelling of judgment.** It now allows the *e* as in the British spelling: *judgement*. Many people, including teachers, don't know about this change.
3. **The dictionary lists *indexes* as the preferred plural for *index* instead of *indices*.** Most people don't know this.

Fortunately, readers aren't very critical. In fact, you're lucky to have them read your letters at all, much less analyze them critically.

To write successful letters today, you need to know what motivates your readers to accept your ideas and to feel good about you.

Most people:

1. **Refuse to read letters longer than one page.** They may pretend to read them—but mostly they lose interest quickly.

2. **Prefer short sentences** (therefore, thirteen to fifteen words would be a good average number) **and paragraphs** (one to three sentences are good; never more than seven lines).

3. **Want to know "what's in it for me" right away.** You should focus on customer benefits up front.

4. **Remember the last thing they read first.** For this reason, dates and action statements belong at the end where they will be remembered.

5. **Are inspired by instant gratification rather than deferred pleasures.** Show quick return on investment whenever you can.

6. **Are turned off when they read fancy-sounding words.** This includes legalistic language and clichés. So you're better off translating the so-called professional language you hear so often in business writing into more conversational words.

   As for clichés, some phrases are so overworked that your reader doesn't even see them on the page.

   > We are sorry for any inconvenience we may have caused you in this matter.

   You may think you sound sincere, but these words are trite and overworked. This passage would be much more convincing:

   > We're sorry for the frustration this delay has caused you. There's no excuse for you to receive anything but excellent service from us.

7. **React poorly to negative or parental language.** In other words, you should never sound as if you are talking down to your readers.

   It's always a good idea to inject a positive note into your writing. Note the difference between these two phrases:

   > We can't ship the blankets you ordered until you send us a check for $200.

* * * * *

> As soon as you send your check for $200, we'll be happy to ship your blankets to you.

You're parental or at least stuffy when you use words like *advise* or *it is our intention*. Substitute *inform* and *we plan* to sound more reader-friendly.

You're also parental when you mention your company name again and again throughout your letter. Using it a few times is fine, but personal pronouns like *we* are preferred.

8. **Have the attention span of a flea and are superlazy.** For this reason, you need to grab readers' attention right away or all your good ideas to follow will be wasted. And you can't have the luxury of throwing in a lot of unnecessary language—not if you want to get your point across.

   One way to cater to today's lazy readers is to use a block style for your letters, where you don't indent for paragraphs and all writing is flush with the left margin. You're better off not indenting for paragraphs in internal documents, too.

9. **Need to be stimulated to act.** How about this ending?

> Hoping to hear from you, I remain.

Of course you remain—you don't go with the letter. As for the first part of the sentence, your readers may well say, "Go on hoping. Maybe I'll get around to responding and maybe I won't."

You can stimulate your readers by providing a date for their response, even if you have to make one up. Don't bother to explain your deadline—just give it.

You can also stimulate readers by using persuasive language, as in this example:

> As soon as you sign the enclosed documents and return them to me, I'll immediately credit your account for $300.

This tells them to get busy.

You never write in a vacuum. Since you're writing to real people, whether you know them or not, you have to anticipate their responses to your words.

Put yourself in their shoes and then walk around in them for a while. How would you react to a phrase or an idea? Chances are, if you wouldn't like it, they wouldn't either.

*　*　*　*　*

This book features two kinds of letters:

1. **Prospecting letters,** where you're persuading readers (often strangers to you) to purchase your goods, services, or ideas.
2. **Account management letters,** where you're explaining, thanking, apologizing, persuading, inquiring, or building goodwill.

In every case, write to win. Pretend your reader is standing beside you, and talk to him or her in a natural, conversational tone.

Good luck—and happy selling!

PART ONE

Techniques for Writing Sales and Account Management Letters

1

Speak Your Reader's Language

Eschew Obfuscation!

—Anonymous

All your letters to customers are sales tools, from cold-contact, prospecting letters to apologies for less-than-perfect service. Each time you write, you want to put your language to work for you—both to establish a relationship and to get results.

To select the most effective language for your letters, your best bet is to analyze who is reading them. Here is a composite picture of today's customers, based on their likes and dislikes.

Profile of Today's Customer

Likes	Dislikes
• Friendly, warm approach	• Intimidating language
• Focus on benefits (what's in it for them)	• Long-winded descriptions of features
• Quick, easy-to-read, sincere tone with purpose stated up front	• Hard-to-read prose with trite, overworked phrases
• A "you" approach	• Narrative (once upon a time) openings
	• A self-centered, "we" approach

Most of us struggle in deciding what tone to use every time we write. But it's particularly important to focus on a winning tone when we're trying to attract customers or keep the ones we have happy.

The following guidelines focus on the needs and interests of your readers.

GUIDELINE 1:
IF YOU WOULDN'T SAY IT, DON'T WRITE IT

Instead of:	Say:
• Pursuant to our discussion . . .	• As we discussed . . .
• I would like to take this opportunity to explain the problems.	• I'd like to explain the problems.
• Should you have any further questions, do not hesitate to call.	• If you have any other questions, please call me.
• Thank you for your cooperation in this matter.	• Thanks for your help in solving my delivery problems.
• In regard to . . .	• Concerning . . .
• It has come to our attention . . .	• [Omit this phrase—it's a time waster.]
• This is to summarize . . .	• I'd like to summarize . . .
• This is to advise . . .	• I'd like to tell you about . . .
• Kindly remit . . .	• Please pay . . .
• Thank you in advance for . . .	• Thank you for . . .
• Thank you for your patronage.	• We're pleased to have your business.

When my two sons were eight and nine, they decided to take advantage of having Brill for a last name. Here's the letter they jointly wrote to the Brillo Company:

Dear Brillo:

How would you like to put our names in lights? Our friends call us pad one and pad two. You could use us in your advertising, and we could all get rich.

The response?

> Gentlemen:
>
> Pursuant to your recent communication, we are unable to utilize you in our advertising campaign due to the restraints of our company policy.

Why would anyone use such stuffy language when writing to children? Maybe the writer wanted to sound important or to seem professional. But what we really need to do is tone down the formality of all our letters, regardless of the age of our readers.

In an issue of the *American Quarterly*, Lionel Trilling bemoans our love affair with jargon. He suggests that eventually people will be unable to say *We fell in love and married*. Here's the unattractive alternative he envisions:

> Their libidinal impulses being reciprocal, they integrated their individual erotic drives and brought them within the same frame of reference.

I'm sure we'd all rather fall in love than integrate drives.

Imagine yourself having a problem with mushrooms sprouting all over your lawn. You write about this problem to a fertilizer company, only to receive this response:

> Dear Mr. Masterson:
>
> The spores to which you have alluded have manifested themselves due to the alkaline quality of your soil.
>
> It is recommended that a mixture of water and Jiffy Mix be utilized on the affected area.

You, like Mr. Masterson, might well decide to find another product to solve your problem—from a company whose language you speak.

GUIDELINE 2:
USE CONTRACTIONS FREELY IN ALL YOUR LETTERS

Forget what your English teacher told you about using contractions in your term papers. They go to work for you, as you can see in these examples.

> Is there something we forgot to do that has kept you from paying your bill? If so, we'll do our part to make it right.

> On the other hand, if we've fulfilled our part of the contract, won't you fulfill yours in return by sending your check for $176 today?

Contractions make you sound conversational.

> How does an all-expense-paid trip to Costa Rica in February sound to you?

> We're pleased to announce this year's P&B Fun in the Sun Sales Contest. We've made it easy for every one of you to win. Here's how it works.

> P&B is launching a special promotion of its new Quickshot camera in August. During the three months the special promotion runs, you'll only need to sell 3,000 cameras—which should be a cinch because of all the exciting new features this product has to offer.

> Here is the itinerary. You'll jet to Costa Rica the second week of February. You will stay at the Hilton for seven sunny, action-packed days. Imagine yourself lolling in the sun when the rest of us are slaving away in ice-cold weather.

> It's a compelling picture, isn't it? We're holding a sales meeting next week to launch the Quickshot. Start thinking Costa Rica—it's in the bag!

Note: As with any rule, don't forget to apply your common sense. Contractions are too informal for some situations (e.g., a letter that you want to appear legal).

GUIDELINE 3:
USE QUESTIONS ANYWHERE IN YOUR LETTERS TO CREATE INTEREST AND GRAB YOUR READER'S ATTENTION

opening line:

Have you heard the latest discount news? As a first-time buyer, you're entitled to a 10% reduction in your mortgage rate.

middle of the letter:

These reproductions are more than just bargain priced; they have set the standard in the industry.

Sounds too good to be true, right? Please bear with me for a moment while I explain why we have made this spectacular offer available.

end of the letter:

Wouldn't it be great if you could control the way your computer screen looks—without leaving your document? Call today and we'll make it happen for you.

GUIDELINE 4:
USE *AND* OR *BUT* TO BEGIN SENTENCES OR EVEN PARAGRAPHS

You can learn a lot from newspaper and magazine ads, where companies research the effect of their words before investing big dollars. These ads regularly use *and* and *but* as openers to create a smooth flow.

Examples of Ad Copy Use of And *and* But

When you sign up for our 7¢-a-minute rate, you can also get a break on all your long-distance calls within the United States. Since you have friends and relatives on both sides of the border, deciding who's going to hear from you first may not be as simple as you thought.

* * * * *

We know that even the greatest competitors need help along the way. That's why this year we're offering you the Gold Star Program. For less than $89 a month, you get a terrific 5900 copier, free copy cartridges, and unlimited copies for a whole year. But hurry—this offer won't last forever.

* * * * *

The loss of your business data could cost you thousands of dollars—or even the business itself. Unless, of course, you have Easyfind. A breakthrough concept, Easyfind is a foolproof, fail-safe, online backup and recovery service. Just set it and forget it. And you'll never have to think about backups again.

* * * * *

But actually, our offer doesn't end there. This Allied credit card comes complete with a whole host of features you're sure to enjoy.

GUIDELINE 5:
GET RID OF THE HYPE

Today's customers are much more sophisticated than ever before—and more knowledgeable. Without some facts to back it up, they're unlikely to accept your claim that your product is the best.

Here's an excerpt from a cover letter to a proposal. The reader rejected the company solely because of the hype, and went with the competition—whose language was readable.

original:

Cross-Town can assist Allied in REDUCING ITS TOW CLAIMS while at the same time providing Allied owners and dealers with a standardized benefit program for warranty-covered disablements, available to Allied dealers and owners 24 hours a day, 365 days a year, wherever and whenever they travel throughout the United States and Canada. Furthermore, this program can be IMPLEMENTED utilizing our existing 24-hour toll-free, exclusive, dedicated Allied Roadside Assistance Lines (exclusive to only Allied owners, Allied dealers, and Allied employees), a number which Allied dealers have already been accustomed to utilizing for the past three plus (3 +) years.

Here are some of the problem areas (besides overall wordiness).

1. Repeating Allied's name so often just gets in the way of the message.
2. Another kind of repetition is redundancy (repeating concepts). Examples above are *while at the same time, exclusive to only,* and *three plus (3 +).*
3. Underlining and bolding should be used sparingly or these techniques will have no effect. Also, it's foolish to underline a passage that's already bold.

Please note what happens when you make the language more concrete and shorten the sentences and paragraphs. Which version would you find more appealing?

rewrite:

First, we'll help you reduce your tow claims. Also, your owners and dealers will enjoy a standardized benefit program for warranty-related problems—available 24 hours a day, 365 days a year, throughout the U.S. and Canada.

You can implement this program by using our exclusive toll-free Allied Roadside Assistance lines. Many of your dealers have been using this number for over three years. We'll be happy to give you a list if you want their reading on what we have to offer.

GUIDELINE 6:
SHORTEN YOUR SENTENCES AND PARAGRAPHS

Shorter sentences provide ease of reading; shorter paragaphs create more white space, which translates into a more attractive page.

Here are two versions of the same letter for you to compare. So far, everyone I have shown these to prefers the second version. See if you agree.

version 1:

It was certainly a pleasure to meet with you and Mr. Churchill on May 1, and we very much appreciated the opportunity to discuss your plans for a review of the Marbach Investment Company and the desirability of developing a systems plan to relate management requirements with systems hardware and software decisions in the future. Our overall impression is that Marbach's data processing and systems operations face several major decisions. The Company must decide in the near future the direction of its hardware and systems efforts in terms of centralized versus distributed processing and the desirability of upgrading your equipment.

As discussed, accurate, meaningful, and timely information is truly vital for successful business operations and the attainment of any company's objectives. We believe systems planning is essential if Marbach is to realize the greatest benefits from its investment in these resources, and we propose to work with the Company to obtain a better focus on information systems requirements and hardware requirements by formally developing a long-range systems plan.

version 2:

We very much enjoyed meeting with you and Mr. Churchill. Thanks for informing us of your plans to review your data processing and for exchanging views on systems planning.

You're facing several major decisions. Do you move toward centralized or distributed processing? How will you revise your major systems using a database? And how will you expand them to service new product lines?

To ensure that these questions are considered as a whole, we strongly recommend systems planning. Your company needs up-to-date and accurate information to survive. To select the "right" system that will yield this information, you must have the strongest systems planning available.

We'd very much like to work with you, and help you form a long-range systems plan that will successfully focus on your systems and hardware requirements.

GUIDELINE 7:
USE ACTIVE, SIMPLE VERBS

Substitute the active voice for the passive whenever possible. Active verbs are more forceful and personal.

passive:

> Your letter of February 4 was referred to me for reply by Gary Halstead. [*The subject receives the action of the verb.*]

active:

> Gary Halstead asked me to respond to your letter of February 4. [*The subject is performing the action.*]

passive:

> Your order will be shipped by air express in order that it may reach you more quickly.

active:

> We are shipping your order by air express so you will receive it quickly.

passive:

> The papers have been reviewed by our Payroll Department.

active:

> Our Payroll Department has reviewed the papers.

However, you do want to use the passive in these situations:

1. When you want to soften your approach and avoid sounding accusatory in sensitive situations.

> The July check was not included in your envelope.

* * * * *

There is an error in the assessment.

2. When you want to sound more cordial, less direct.

You are invited to participate in our upcoming symposium.

GUILDELINE 8:
TRANSLATE VERBS INTO THEIR SIMPLEST FORMS

For some reason, we seem to feel it's more professional to extend our verbs or to change them into another part of speech.

Verbs are the strongest elements in the English language. By using them, you inject energy into your writing.

instead of:

We have made a careful analysis of your account.

say:

We have carefully analyzed your account.

instead of:

We are in need of more information from you.

say:

We need more information from you.

instead of:

Our vitamins will make a dramatic change in the way you feel.

say:

Our vitamins will dramatically improve the way you feel.

instead of:

It is our recommendation that you purchase the whole package.

say:

We recommend that you purchase the whole package.

instead of:

This product will make an improvement in your turnaround time of 20%.

say:

> This product will improve your turnaround time by 20%.

instead of:

> These changes have been made in the blueprints for the elimination of inaccurate information.

say:

> We have changed the blueprints to eliminate inaccurate information.

The last point about verbs involves our tendency to change them into nouns.

Stronger	Weaker
develop	development
apply	application
approve	approval
determine	determination
recommend	recommendation
discuss	discussion

Compare these sentences:

> After we conducted an investigation into your payment history, we made a recommendation to our Payroll staff about eliminating the charges from your account.

> After reviewing your payment history, we asked Payroll to remove the charges from your account.

* * * * *

> We came to an agreement about how we can best effect changes in our programs.

> We agreed on the best ways to improve our programs.

* * * * *

Our manager came to the conclusion that our sales force can achieve great improvements in its numbers by making arrangements for more sales calls.

Our manager concluded that our sales force can improve its numbers by making more sales calls.

* * * * *

We are in need of improvements in our procedures.

We need to improve our procedures.

2

Give Your Readers What They Want

The only way I can get you to do anything is by giving you what you want.

—Dale Carnegie

You may think you are selling a product or service in your letters, but you're really selling benefits to your customer. So your greatest motivator is an appeal to your reader's self-interest.

The first question we ask in reading a sales letter is "What's in it for me?" You can best answer that question by being reader-centered, not self-centered.

GUIDELINE 1:
KEY IN ON YOUR READER'S PRIME MOTIVATORS

Negative Motivators

These may play upon the readers' fears so they will see your product in a favorable light, as in the following example.

negative appeal:

Downsizing, rightsizing . . . it's all the same. And it could well affect you.

* * * * *

One way to maintain a competitive edge in your workplace is to dress for success. At the Mart, we have just the choice of clothing and expert sales advisers that can guarantee success for you.

Other fears you might use as the basis of a sales appeal are sickness, poverty, crime, loss of property, guilt, or anger.

These openers for prospecting letters typify a negative appeal:

These are tough times.

* * * * *

You worry about your family's health. So do we.

* * * * *

Annoying, isn't it? Every time you park your car, you're not sure if it will still be there when you return.

The following phrases motivate through a suggested penalty for not purchasing now.

Only some can qualify.

* * * * *

Last time, this product sold out.

* * * * *

We only have a limited number available.

* * * * *

There's a penalty for delay.

* * * * *

The last time we offered this special promotion we had to disappoint over 300 customers—we just didn't have enough to go around.

* * * * *

Why wait for the mail? Call today to ensure that your makeup package will still be available.

Positive Motivators

Motivator	Possible Openers for Prospecting Letter
Convenience or comfort:	Imagine yourself relaxing in your favorite easy chair . . . with our book at your side.
Profit or money savings:	If I could show you how to double your income, would you be interested?
Time savings:	I won't waste your time—but I will tell you how to save it.
Increased pleasure:	You want it . . . and we can get it for you.
Love or friendship:	You're important to us.
Status:	We're pleased to make you part of a select group to receive this offer.
Health and well-being:	Would you snap up a pill that promised you eternal life? Well, we can't offer you one, but we do have a vitamin that will make you feel eternal.
Improved appearance:	So much has been promised about weight loss lately. Like you, I'm a doubter. Let's be realistic for a minute about what we can do for you.
Common ground:	Over 5,000 doctors have already signed up for our service.
Intelligence:	It's a competitive world out there, and few schools are up to the task of readying your children to succeed.
	Our reading program can raise any child's scores by at least one grade level—guaranteed.

Writing to the reader's needs and interests is known as a *you* attitude (as opposed to a self-centered *we* attitude).

"we" attitude:

> I would like to take this opportunity to express my appreciation for the account you have opened. It is our intention to offer a full range of services for our customers.

"you" attitude:

> Thank you for opening an account with us. Serving you for all your shopping needs will be a pleasure.

"we" attitude:

> We need you to help us bring our records up-to-date by sending us the information we have requested on the enclosed form.

"you" attitude:

> Please fill out and return the enclosed form so you'll be sure to receive our important information promptly.

"we" attitude:

> We notice from our records that we still have not received payment owed us of $140.

"you" attitude:

> You still owe us $140.

The "you" attitude is expressed in an anonymous writer's analysis of the most important words in the English language.

Five words:	*I am proud of you.*
Four words:	*What do you think?*
Three words:	*If you please, . . .*
Two words:	*Thank you.*
One word:	*You . . .*

The following letter segment, which the Postal Service wrote to a customer whose package was lost, certainly doesn't have a "you" focus.

Thank you for letting us know about your lost package to your aunt. U.S. Postal Service handles millions of packages a day, and only .001 percent are ever lost.

All this letter succeeds in doing is to make the customer feel even worse that she was so unlucky. Why be self-serving in dealing with problems? Here is how the writer might have begun this letter.

We share your concern that your package never reached your aunt. Here's what we can do to help.

An automobile manufacturer wrote the following letter to its customers, explaining a recall.

Sounds as if Paragon is reluctant.
As a responsible company, Paragon Motorworks feels an <u>obligation</u> to address our customers' concerns, which is why Paragon recently announced a program to recall 7.2 million vehicles for the purpose of replacing their ignition switches. While the actual number of com-
Who can figure this out?
plaints was less than <u>two hundredths of one percent</u>, it is important that these concerns <u>be properly addressed</u>.
passive

Wouldn't you rather receive this rewrite?

Your concerns and driving satisfaction are important to us. That's why we recently started a program to recall over seven million vehicles to replace their ignition switches.

The actual number of complaints has been quite small—fewer than one out of every 20,000 customers. But we want to make sure that you're a happy and comfortable Paragon car owner.

GUIDELINE 2:
FOCUS ON CUSTOMER BENEFITS

You're much more persuasive by showing the benefits of your product, service, or idea than by just explaining the features.

feature:

We have a 24-hour hot line.

benefit:

Our 24-hour hot line will ensure that you'll have all your questions answered right away.

When you're describing benefits, avoid using abstract language, as in the following example:

abstract:

Gordon Sales and Marketing can help advertisers speak to their customers by providing local marketing opportunities that tie directly into their business.

concrete:

We can help you communicate with your customers by finding you local contacts directly related to your business.

If you incorporate the words *so* and *because* into your sales writing, you may find it easier to describe benefits.

Our widget has three central drive shafts so you can operate your machinery one-third faster.

* * * * *

You'll have easier access to your sales force because we have installed three new terminals.

By offering tangible benefits like givebacks or anything "value added" to your customers, you create a particularly strong appeal. Coupons work well today because they are tangible and immediate.

Still, your most effective tool is your choice of language. You can see a major difference in these versions of the same letter.

vague promise:

I am interested in discussing with you how Artistry, Inc., can save you time and money in all your printing. I would appreciate the opportunity of meeting with you in order that I might demonstrate all that we have to offer.

concrete promise:

Can you spare five minutes to hear how Artistry, Inc., can save you time and money on all your printing? Here's a sample of what we have to offer.

- At least 15% faster processing time than you're getting now.
- A minimum of 5% less in cost of reproductions.
- Discounts on color that I think will really surprise you.

If you think these benefits—and several others I have to offer—are worth five minutes of your time, please take my phone call Tuesday morning. As the expression says, "Can we talk?"

GUIDELINE 3:
PERSONALIZE YOUR LETTERS

The best way to personalize is to use personal pronouns like *you*, *I*, or *we*. Your company's name is on the letterhead. You won't create extra awareness of your company by repeating this name mindlessly throughout the letter, as we believed years ago. Instead, repeating your company's name makes you seem impersonal, and you'll just annoy your reader, as in the next example.

impersonal:

Dear Ms. Cross:

As a result of the tax research recently completed by Interwell, it has been determined that Interwell is liable for collecting Colorado State sales tax on all interstate telecommunication services billed to our customers. Therefore, on your June 1997 Interwell invoice, under the section marked "Private Services," there is a sales charge in the amount of $324.04.

personal:

Dear Ms. Cross:

I'd like to explain a sales charge on your June 1997 invoice that you may find confusing. We're responsible for collecting Colorado State sales tax for any telecommunication services that we bill to you. That's why you'll see a charge of $324.04 under the section marked "Private Services."

Use personal pronouns anywhere in your letters to create a friendly atmosphere.

instead of:

It is recommended . . .

try:

We recommend . . .

instead of:

It is our hope . . .

try:

We hope . . .

instead of:

The enclosed guidelines should be reviewed.

try:

Please review the enclosed guidelines [*"you" is understood as the subject of review*].

A powerful way to personalize is to mention your reader's name once in the body of your letter, either by last name (for a more formal letter) or first name.

Dear Ms. Cornelio:

When my manager suggested that I ask a few customers how they feel about our service, I immediately thought of you, Ms. Cornelio. You're an excellent customer, so I'm especially interested in your opinion.

Would you please take a moment to check off the answers to the few questions below? Just drop the form in the mail, using the enclosed prepaid envelope.

If you do it today, I'll be doubly grateful. Thanks so much for your help.

I like the use of a personal note—handwritten—after your signature.

> *I think you'll find page 22 of the brochures particularly interesting, Frank—it outlines the new color options we discussed.*

Why not try handwriting a note in the margin, right next to an idea you want to highlight? Keep this short, something like *Great cost savings!*

It's very important to personalize your salutation, even if you don't know your reader. Throw out dull, stodgy phrases like *To whom it may concern* or *Dear Sir*. Actually, assuming you're writing to a man is both politically incorrect and offensive. And *Dear Sir/Madam* is not much better.

So what do you do when you're writing to a group or to someone you don't know? Write to a title. Here are some possibilities:

Dear Personnel Manager	Dear Vacationer
Dear Investor	Dear Member
Dear Golf Lover	Dear Applicant
Dear Business Traveler	Dear Business Owner
Dear Reader	Dear Valued Customer
Dear Contributor	Dear Animal Lover
Dear Friend	

Note: Europeans still use *Gentlemen* or *Dear Sir* freely in their business letters.

If you don't like writing to a title, you can substitute a phrase for the salutation (placing it in the same place you would put the salutation, just after the address).

Ms. Margie Murstein
1242 Main Street
Anywhere, New York 12000

Just so you know . . .

The bad news is that we have just eliminated three products from our line. The good news is that we've replaced them with some terrific new widgets—that I think you're going to love.

Note that the punctuation is flexible for this nontraditional substitute salutation. In business letters, we usually use a colon after the salutation. In sales letters, we sometimes use a comma after a person's name to seem more personal (not that it's correct—but remember, if it works, then it's fine). The following examples use different kinds of punctuation.

Nontraditional Punctuation in Salutations

We believe you'll be pleased with your decision . . .

* * * * *

Congratulations on your new home!

* * * * *

Welcome to The Mart!

* * * * *

You're right . . .

* * * * *

We need your help:

* * * * *

I think we should meet . . .

* * * * *

You did an excellent job, Sam . . .

Other Techniques for Personalizing Letters

1. Include an inked-on signature on computer-generated letters.
2. Use a stamp instead of metered mail.
3. Make the letter look home-typed.
4. Add specific phrases to your form letters. For example, say *Thank you for telling us about the broken pottery* instead of *Thank you for informing us about your problem.*

GUIDELINE 4:
DON'T GO OVERBOARD IN TRYING TO BE FRIENDLY

Personal is good. Cute, on the other hand, may alienate rather than amuse. Here are some openings that are questionable, at best.

too informal for many readers:

Ouch! Our faces sure are red!

* * * * *

We goofed! [*Again, as much as we've relaxed our approach to language, this may go too far for many readers.*]

* * * * *

Trust us. . . . You won't be sorry!

By the way, use exclamation points sparingly in your account management letters. They may make your letter sound like a marketing tool rather than a personal expression. Save the drama for prospecting letters.

GUIDELINE 5:
GET YOUR CUSTOMER'S NAME AND GENDER RIGHT

One of the biggest turnoffs in receiving a letter is to see your name spelled incorrectly or to be addressed by the wrong gender title.

Francis Peabody was infuriated at having a company representative write to him as Ms. Peabody when the spelling of his first name clearly indicates he's a man (other names aren't so clearly differentiated).

When he wrote that he couldn't do business with a company that couldn't be bothered to get his gender right, he received the following letter in response.

Humorous Apology

Dear Mr. Peabody:

We share your concern that our employee Rebecca Stringdale mistook you for a woman. There's no excuse for this kind of carelessness.

Rest assured it will never happen again. We took Rebecca out and shot her at dawn. Will you give us another chance?

While attempts at humor are often perceived as sarcasm or sometimes fall flat, if the client is about to drop you anyway, you have nothing to lose. In Mr. Peabody's case, it was certainly a wise decision to try a humorous approach. He chuckled for a bit and then gave the company another chance.

It's hard to deal with some of the complex gender issues we face today. Of course the best approach is to take the time to call if you're unsure. Second-best would be to take no chances.

If you receive a letter from Sam Brown, and you have no clue whether this Sam is a man or a woman, try a salutation that says *Dear Sam Brown*.

For other gender issues, you have two options.

1. Acknowledge that women exist by using either *his/her* or *his or her*, as in these examples:

   Every sales manager should ask his or her staff to revise their schedules.

   Please have each customer service rep change his/her price lists.

2. Make everything plural to avoid the awkwardness of recognizing the two genders. Here is an example.

   Please have all sales managers revise their schedules.

Please note the following distinctions:

	Awkward	Preferred
Politically incorrect:	Each customer should be aware of his options.	Each customer should be aware of his or her options.
Grammatically wrong:	Each customer should be aware of their options ["*customer*" *is singular, so* "*their*" *can't modify it*].	All customers should be aware of their options.

GUIDELINE 6:
ESTABLISH TRUST

With so many exaggerated claims being made today and so much cynicism evidenced by customers, the company that sounds sincere and believable is a winner every time.

It may even be a good idea to admit a small weakness in

your product just so the rest of your claim sounds worthy of trust.

> We're a bit pricey, but we're worth it.

Which of these phrases sounds more believable to you?

> You will be completely satisfied!

> I believe you will be very satisfied.

* * * * *

> It's the opportunity of your life!

> I think you will find this is an excellent opportunity.

* * * * *

> We're taking precautions to prevent this from happening again.

> We're alerting customer service to watch your account to ensure you don't get double-billed again.

* * * * *

> I'm sure you have heard . . .

> Have you heard . . . ?

* * * * *

> We have notified the appropriate party for resolution.

> I'm referring your complaint to our service manager, Susan Patek. She will get back to you within a week.

Ten Ways to Establish Trust

1. Offer guarantees on your products or service.
2. Try a money-back offer.

3. Offer to let customers keep a bonus gift, even if they don't want the product.
4. Don't downgrade the competition.
5. Use specific language. Instead of *We can improve your ratings,* say, *We can increase your ratings by 10%.*
6. Tell your customers when they are right.
7. Cite the number of years you've been in business.
8. Offer testimonials from happy customers.
9. Mention by name sample customers who are happy with you.
10. Acknowledge concerns with sincerity: *We're as concerned as you are that . . .*

3

Be Positive (Even When You Must Say No), and Build Goodwill

I always try to keep my words soft, honeyed, and warm because I never know when I will be called upon to eat them.

—*Senator Everett Dirkson*

BE POSITIVE

Words and phrases carry positive or negative overtones. To appeal to your reader, keep your language as upbeat as you can.

Language That Appeals

attractive	select	perfect
exclusive	superior	new
exceptional	worthwhile	best
success	proven	satisfy
guarantee	love	enjoy
value	money	
easy	results	
instant	save	
free	special	
plus	latest	

Language That Annoys

We regret to inform . . .	I don't agree with you that . . .
You have failed to . . .	I must question . . .
You claim/contend . . .	We do not understand why . . .
We are afraid that . . .	Your account is delinquent . . .
We have been unsuccessful . . .	We must delay . . .

Language Translations

negative:

Don't miss this opportunity.

positive:

Take this opportunity.

negative:

Don't forget to . . .

positive:

Remember to . . .

negative:

I can't.

positive:

I wish I could.

negative:

If you send . . .

positive:

When you send . . .

negative:

You can't have _____ until you _____ .

positive:

You can have _____ as soon as you _____ .

negative:

Please advise us if _____ is incorrect.

positive:

Please let us know if _____ is correct.

negative:

Your _____ won't be ready until . . .

positive:

We can promise to send you _____ by _____ .

negative:

We make no refunds following the warranty period.

positive:

We can only make refunds during the guarantee period.

negative:

We must deny payment of your claim as the injury did not prevent your return to work within 24 hours.

positive:

Since you returned to work the same day as your injury, your claim is denied.

negative:

If you do not pay your bill for $200, your credit will be damaged.

positive:

You can ensure that your credit rating stays positive by paying us $200 now.

negative:

I'm sorry there was an incorrect charge on your account.

positive:

We've already corrected the mistake on your account. Thanks for letting us know about it, and for your patience with us.

negative:

Our warranty doesn't cover normal wear and tear.

positive:

Our warranty covers everything except normal wear and tear.

negative:

You neglected to include a color choice in your order.

positive:

Please let us know what color you want so we can complete your order.

negative:

I'm sorry we weren't able to send the sofa you recently ordered, but we have discontinued that line.

positive:

I wish I could fill your recent order, but we no longer stock the model you wanted.

negative:

We are canceling your account as you haven't paid your bill for $340.

positive:

You can reinstate your account by paying $340 now.

Positive Openers When the News Is Bad

Your interest in Allied Services is admirable, and I'm impressed with your commitment. Unfortunately, . . .

* * * * *

We're as upset as you are that . . .

* * * * *

I wish I could participate in the upcoming symposium. From your literature, it sounds like a winner.

* * * * *

I enjoyed reading your proposal and found your ideas very interesting. Unfortunately, . . .

* * * * *

I'd like to explain our position concerning _____ .

* * * * *

We have carefully considered your excellent suggestion on how we handle returns. We wish we could . . .

* * * * *

I certainly understand how you must have felt when. . . . However, may I explain why we reached this decision?

* * * * *

We appreciate your interest in _____ .

* * * * *

Mark Fitzgerald shared your letter with me and asked me to reply on his behalf.

* * * * *

The last thing I want to write to you about is a price increase. But . . .

* * * * *

Old friends like you are the best friends . . . so I was concerned to learn we haven't heard from you in over a year.

* * * * *

I share your concern about the _____ .

* * * * *

Is there some reason you haven't responded to our last three collection notices?

* * * * *

Is there some reason you haven't sent us the brochures you promised on June 14?

* * * * *

I wish we could accept your application for a _____ .

Positive Closings When the News Is Bad

Although we can't offer you a donation right now, we applaud your efforts.

* * * * *

My compliments to you on your worthwhile project. I wish more people shared your feelings.

* * * * *

I wish I could join you at your convention. Good luck with your dynamic program.

* * * * *

Right now our funds are earmarked for other projects. We wish you the best of luck.

* * * * *

Thanks for letting us consider your project. I wish you success in completing it.

* * * * *

We appreciate your alerting us to our mailing problem and your taking the time to write.

* * * * *

We appreciate your patience with us. As a small token of our apology, please accept next month's bill on us—It's the least we can do.

* * * * *

Thanks for your understanding. We'll certainly do our best to give you the excellent service you deserve from now on.

* * * * *

I'm optimistic we can settle this problem within the next week.

* * * * *

I think we've solved the problem. But if anything else comes up, please call me directly at 555-4545.

* * * * *

We're always eager to hear all your comments and suggestions.

* * * * *

We'll be happy to reimburse you for any expenses this delay may have caused. Please send your bill marked to my attention, and I'll take care of it right away.

* * * * *

Thanks for bearing with us during these difficult days.

* * * * *

We're pleased we've been able to solve this problem so quickly. We couldn't have done it without your support.

Positive No Letter-1

Your request that I speak to your group on August 10 is flattering. I appreciate your invitation.

Unfortunately, I'll be out of town on that date. May I suggest an alternative? Marta Fernandez has been with Acme for over 15 years. She has a diverse background in motivational speaking and would be happy to fill in if you need her.

If you'd like to speak with Marta, you can reach her at 555-1111.

Once again, I appreciate your thinking of me.

Positive No Letter-2

In going over your résumé, I was impressed with your background and skills.

Right now, we've filled all our open positions. However, something may come up later, and we'll be happy to keep your résumé in our six-month file in case we find something appropriate.

Good luck with your job search.

Positive No Letter-3

We appreciate your recent request for a discount when you order in bulk from us. Actually, you're already receiving a substantial discount— at least 15% off what our competitors charge. So our prices are low every time you order.

Thanks for your letter. We always enjoy hearing from you.

Positive No Letter Explaining the Reason for Saying No

We're as upset as you are that your furniture order has been delayed. The good news is that this style is so popular. The bad news is that we've had trouble keeping up with the orders.

Bill Stanton, our service manager, says the holdup seems to be in the factory. Bill has promised me a firm commitment by January 14. You'll receive your items by January 20 (or earlier, if possible).

Thanks for your patience. We think your couch and chairs will be well worth the short extra wait.

Positive Denial of Funds

I appreciate your recent request for a contribution to the Wildlife Preservation Fund. I can think of no more worthwhile undertaking.

I wish I could say yes to you. But right now, our funds are earmarked for other projects.

I wish you the best of luck with your campaign.

Starting Positive, Then Saying No

Your suggestion to use bubble protector sheets in all our packages was well thought out. It makes good sense.

Right now we're looking for ways to cut down on our shipping and handling costs. So we're holding off on any changes in our shipping procedures.

We always appreciate helpful customers like you, Mr. Skye. Thanks so much for taking the time to write.

* * * * *

To sound less confrontational, you may choose to use the passive voice. That way, you deliberately avoid being too personal, as in the following examples.

Because the claim is still open, the payment must be postponed.

* * * * *

If the warranty extended beyond two years, your transmission would still be covered.

* * * * *

The claim is disallowed because of the warranty lapse.

* * * * *

Your credit history suggests a need for a more solid record of payment. For this reason, the credit request is denied.

* * * * *

Your payment was not received within the discount period, so $55 is the correct charge.

* * * * *

There was no check included in your letter. I'm sure this was just an oversight.

* * * * *

There is no warranty on our tires that covers damage caused by accidents.

Being Positive Without Sounding Pushy

weak:

As you know . . .

better:

As you may know . . .

weak:

I'm sure you have heard . . .

better:

Have you heard? . . .

weak:

I'm sure you'll agree that our product will save you money.

better:

I think you'll enjoy our cost savings.

Avoiding the Word Hope

weak:

We hope you'll agree that our solution is the best one available.

better:

We think you'll agree that our solution is the best one available.

weak:

We hope you will call with any questions.

better:

Any questions? Please call me anytime.

weak:

We hope you will pay the charge by April 1.

better:

Please send your payment of $223 by April 1 so we can settle your account in time for our May sale.

BUILD GOODWILL

Appreciation for business and a thank-you for a good working relationship are just two of the many kinds of goodwill letters you can write. Take a moment also to congratulate customers or coworkers when there's good news.

Thank-You for Business

When we receive a gift, we respond by saying "thank you." Is this a usual practice? Absolutely.

What isn't a usual practice is remembering to thank loyal customers like you. And this is exactly what we should do more often.

Thank you, Ms. Meltzer, for your trust in us and for your repeated business. It's a pleasure to work with you.

Thank-You to a Colleague

Marla—

Your ability and professionalism came through. You cut the time for my clients to complete their paperwork in half—making the closing a snap for all of us.

Thanks for everything.

Appreciation for Business

With the new year almost upon us, we'd like you to know how much we've appreciated your business during the past year.

You have paid your account on time, and you've been courteous in all aspects of your dealings with us.

That's why we'd like to say THANKS, Mr. Bronson—and to wish you a happy and prosperous New Year.

Thank-You for Hospitality

Your thoughtfulness made my recent trip to San Francisco most enjoyable.

From the tour of your plant (what an impressive operation!) to my dinner with you and Anne (terrific food plus great company), the experience couldn't have been better.

Thanks, Paul, for everything. By the way, please remember my offer. If you ever come to New York, I'm ready and eager to show you the town.

Congratulations on a Customer's New Child

I was delighted to hear about the birth of your son. There's no more joyous—or exciting—event than the arrival of your first child.

My best wishes to you and Lois.

Congratulations on a Customer's New Home

Congratulations on your new home purchase. As exciting as this event is, I know the coming weeks will be hectic for you.

If you can use an extra pair of hands to run an errand or pack a box or two, just give me a call. I'll be glad to help.

Congratulations on a Colleague's New Job-1

I was delighted to read in the *Globe* last week about your new position with Allied Advertising.

Allied is known for attracting the best, but they are even luckier to get you.

Enjoy the new work. I know you'll be great!

Congratulations on a Colleague's New Job-2

For once the best person got the job! So congratulations, Frank, on your recent promotion. I can think of no one more deserving of reward. You must be very gratified with your accomplishment.

I'm proud of you and want you to know you'll have my continued support in your new position.

4

Use Your Opening to Capture Your Reader's Attention

If you don't get the reader's attention in the first paragraph, the rest of your message is lost.

—Public relations maxim

Try using the AIM formula to help organize your letters.

A   is for capturing *attention*.
I   is for creating *interest*.
M   is for *motivation* to act.

Attention and interest are discussed in the following sections. Motivation is discussed in Chapter 5.

A IS FOR *ATTENTION*

The first sentence of the letter acts as a hook—a way to compel your reader to move on to the heart of your message. Here are some openers that state the purpose of the letter up front, using the "you centered" approach.

Responding to a Customer's Question or Concern

Here is the information you requested in your letter of June 4. You are certainly correct in thinking we have changed our line of fishing rods and reels.

* * * * *

Thank you for your letter of March 2, requesting information about our prices. We're pleased to enclose a list as of January '97.

* * * * *

You asked about _____ in your recent letter. We're pleased to give you this information.

* * * * *

Your letter asking about our training program raised some interesting points.

* * * * *

You raised some important points in your letter of September 18, and I'd like to review them with you.

* * * * *

You raised some excellent questions about our recent merger. I hope these answers will help avoid any confusion.

Q: *How will the name change affect me?*
A: It won't. Just make out your checks to Home Lending (if you forget and write them to our former name, that's no problem).

Q: *Will my mortgage rate change?*
A: All terms of your agreement stay the same, including your payment rates.

Q: *Can I still prepay anytime I choose?*
A: Absolutely.

* * * * *

You asked about our new line of halogen lightbulbs.

Here's a copy of our recent catalog, with our thanks for your interest.

* * * * *

We are glad to tell you that our service department has found nothing seriously wrong with your toaster oven.

* * * * *

When we received your letter this morning, we immediately checked your account as you suggested.

* * * * *

We're shipping your order today. You should have your books by Tuesday morning at the latest.

* * * * *

In your May 3 letter, you asked about eliminating the service charges from your bill. We've already done this for you.

* * * * *

We've already corrected the error you alerted us to in your letter of July 7.

Saying Thank You

I'm so glad we had a chance to chat yesterday. I appreciate all your helpful suggestions about our project.

* * * * *

Your extra efforts to make our sales meeting a success were evident— and very much appreciated.

* * * * *

Thanks to your helpful suggestions, we've saved $2,000 in the last three months.

* * * * *

You certainly saved the day for us by shipping the calculators air express. Thanks for your quick response.

* * * * *

No one could have worked harder to ensure our project's success. Thanks, Tom. We all appreciate your help.

* * * * *

Your last year's contribution to our safe driving campaign allowed us to save lives. You should congratulate yourself for making a difference.

* * * * *

What a treat it was to receive the delicious basket of Christmas goodies you sent to our office.

* * * * *

It was a pleasure meeting with you yesterday to go over your business needs. Your operation is quite impressive.

* * * * *

Thanks for letting us know about our error in the reservations we made for you. There's no excuse for this kind of mistake.

* * * * *

Thank you so much for our productive meeting this week. I enjoyed our conversation and believe we have a lot to offer your business.

* * * * *

Thank you for your time today and for your enthusiasm about putting our routers to work for you. I'm drafting a proposal now for you to review.

* * * * *

I'm happy to welcome you as a new customer of Allied Limited. Thanks for your order, Ms. Fischer.

* * * * *

Your manufacturing problems are certainly complex, and I was pleased to have the chance to discuss how Anodyne can help you solve them. Here's what I know we can do for you . . . plus a few possibilities as well.

* * * * *

It's an understatement to say how delighted I am to have won your account. Thank you, Alicia, for the part you played in this process.

* * * * *

I appreciate our recent meeting to discuss the Hamilton project. You asked a few questions, and I'm happy to follow up with these answers.

* * * * *

Thank you for your letter letting me know about the upcoming convention in Hawaii. It was so kind of you to take the time when you knew I would be interested.

* * * * *

Just a brief note to thank you for the recommendation you gave me last week. Your thoughts were a big help in getting me the job I wanted. I really appreciate your help.

* * * * *

Just a note to let you know how much your hard work and enthusiasm were appreciated this past year.

* * * * *

Thanks so much for referring Joanne Baker to me as a customer. I certainly appreciate your thoughtfulness and promise to justify your confidence in me.

Requesting Help

I'm sure you'll understand our frustration with your hotel when you hear my story.

* * * * *

We need your help to solve a problem we're having with the IRS.

* * * * *

We're sorry to have to call on you for your help, but we're having a problem with your payroll department.

* * * * *

Would you please answer a simple question for us?

* * * * *

May I ask your help with a problem I'm having?

* * * * *

I had a problem recently with one of your salesmen. Here's what happened.

When You Lose a Customer

Although we tried hard to prevent it, your subscription to *Food* has expired. And now, unfortunately, all the tantalizing pleasures our magazine used to bring you are gone.

* * * * *

We've missed you. . . .

And we're wondering if we have somehow done something to upset you.

Handling Sensitive Issues

I'm sure you'll understand our concern when you read this letter. And from the glowing references we've received about your company, I'm equally sure you'll do the right thing.

* * * * *

Is there some reason you haven't responded to our last letter?

* * * * *

We're concerned about the problems you raised in your last letter.

* * * * *

We share your concern about the delays in your shipment.

* * * * *

You're right. We did forget to send the brochures we promised.

* * * * *

You raised some important concerns in your letter of November 18. I'd like to respond to them in order.

* * * * *

I'm concerned about the bill you sent us for our new carpets.

* * * * *

You were right and we were wrong.

* * * * *

It's a big help to hear from customers when things aren't exactly as expected.

Referring to a Discussion

As we discussed this morning, we need to change our shipping procedures.

* * * * *

I'd like to summarize some of the points we agreed to this morning.

* * * * *

We discussed so many things during our meeting this morning that I'd like to summarize the key points.

* * * * *

You raised some important points during our talk yesterday. I'd like to respond to each in turn.

Reference From Someone Else

Jack Mitchell of our customer service department gave me your letter. He asked me to explain why your order was delayed.

* * * * *

You recently wrote to Gladys Rosner about your problems with our cable system. I'd be happy to respond to the questions you raised.

Flattery

Thank you for the interest you expressed in how we select our fabrics. We're flattered that so successful a distributor would ask our advice.

* * * * *

You've got a winner—one of the best widgets in the industry.

* * * * *

Most people couldn't have done what you have. We're proud of you.

* * * * *

Your marketing proposal is a great piece of analysis—and very well documented. Congratulations on your fine work.

Announcement

Starting April 17, the days on which we can accept clothing donations will change.

* * * * *

Announcing a breakthrough in hair replacement. . . . It's new and it's available to you.

* * * * *

For your information, we've opened a new branch in White Plains. It's a different address, but our service and excellent product line are as fine as ever.

* * * * *

I have good news . . . and more good news for you.

* * * * *

This is important news, so please read this information carefully.

* * * * *

We're moving . . . but only our address has changed.

* * * * *

Our new sales representative, Margo Ames, will be calling on you soon.

* * * * *

We're pleased to let you know about a new product that can make you feel at least ten years younger.

Other Openings You Can Choose

You asked about _____ in your letter. We've been able to . . .

* * * * *

Did you ever receive the check we sent on April 10?

* * * * *

When we received your letter this morning, we immediately checked our files as you suggested.

* * * * *

You'll be pleased to know your account is up-to-date, as you suggested in your letter of November 4.

* * * * *

I'm happy to answer your questions about our payment policies.

* * * * *

Is there some reason we haven't heard from you about _____?

* * * * *

I'm delighted to send you this letter about _____ .

Techniques for Opening Prospecting Letters

Questions are effective attention grabbers when you're writing cold-contact letters. The ones that suggest a yes response are particularly effective.

Questions

question:

Have you ever wished you could be your own boss?

follow-up:

I stopped wishing I could and finally did something about it. Here's how you can do the same.

question:

Do you believe in the saying "The early bird gets the worm"?

follow-up:

You're smart if you do. Four out of every five ideas succeed solely because someone thought of them first.

question:

Just once, wouldn't you like to eat whatever you want—whenever you want it?

follow-up:

You can . . . and not just once, when you sign up for our Trimline plan.

question:

Do you work harder than your CEO?

follow-up:

You bet you do. And there are three reasons you're working harder than you should.

question:

Are you selling as much as you'd like to? Do you think you could do better?

follow-up:

I have a great idea I think will help.

Quotations

You may want to begin with a quotation, as in the following examples.

It was Harry Truman who said, "If you can't stand the heat, stay out of the kitchen." I'll go one further: "If you're afraid of a little risk, then this deal just isn't for you."

But if you're willing to invest a little money for a chance at a big reward, then please read on.

* * * * *

"Carpe diem (seize the day)." —Horace, 65 B.C.

This is the day you finally stop watching everyone else grab the golden ring. Make this the day you finally take control of your own destiny.

In just two short months, you could be on your way to early retirement. Here's how.

* * * * *

"In two words: Im-possible." —Samuel Goldwyn

Walk in our door, and you'll hear two very different words: "can do." You want it—we'll get it for you.

Telling a Story

Another popular technique for this kind of letter is to tell a story connected to your product or service. Here are two examples.

Nancy Whitehall swore she would never buy a computer. It was just too "space age complicated" for her.

And then one day she just happened to find herself at one of our Compu-core stores. And here's what happened to all her preconceptions. All but one disappeared.

Want to know which one didn't change? Computers still aren't cheap. BUT we made Nancy a deal she couldn't refuse.

* * * * *

Twenty years ago, my neighbor and I graduated from the same college. And while we didn't know each other then, we've since become great friends.

Recently we went back for our reunion. We went through the usual litany of children, hobbies, and career. Everything was quite similar until we got to career.

Ted's a middle-level manager working ten hours a day, struggling to keep up with each mortgage payment. I retired last year, with enough money for luxury the rest of my life.

Why did I succeed?

I'm not smarter than Ted, and I wasn't all that dedicated. And I won't call it luck.

I took advantage of my opportunities.

And that is why I'm writing to you and people like you.

Common Openers for Prospecting Letters

looking for:

Looking for a mutual fund that will offer you higher yields?

* * * * *

If you're looking for a group to work with on the Blair project, I'd appreciate the chance to talk with you first.

what if?

What if you had met Hitler before he changed the course of history? It's hard to know how you'll react to any situation until you're in the middle of it.

most will buy:

Only a small number have received this invitation, and we expect most will take advantage of the outstanding cost savings.

they didn't think I could:

They laughed when I said I would own my own company by the time I was forty, but look who's getting the last laugh now.

how to:

How to lose at least ten pounds in one month's time.

if you:

If you're like me, you hate to throw money away. If you could use some help lowering your monthly bills, here's an easy solution.

thousands now:

Thousands now pay a third less in taxes than they did before they read my book.

give me your time or give our product a try:

Give me an hour of your time, and I'll have you speed-reading like a pro.

* * * * *

This letter will only take a minute—but it's an important minute.

* * * * *

Why have we included a sample of our detergent with this letter? Because I'm so sure that if you try it once, you'll become an enthusiastic customer right away.

I have to admit:

I won't lie to you. Our prices are up a bit. But there's a good reason for that.

before you:

Before you decide which telephone company will design a custom setup for you, there are a few things you should know about us.

wouldn't it be great. . . ?

Wouldn't it be great if you could afford a house with all the features you're looking for? If you could have someone else do all the maintenance work?

have you ever wished. . . ?

Have you ever wished you could bake like a pro? Imagine yourself creating elegant pies and cakes to the applause of family and friends.

have you noticed. . . ?

Have you noticed how many people talk on a cellular phone these days? What does this mean?

Creative Openers You Can Play With

Nobody has enough money.

* * * * *

Don't try to save money. Let us do it for you.

* * * * *

It may sound too good to be true, but we're ready to . . .

* * * * *

You're the best. And you deserve the best.

* * * * *

Can we talk?

* * * * *

I'm mad . . . and I'm not going to take it anymore.

* * * * *

If you knew you had one year to live . . .

* * * * *

Do you hate your computer?

* * * * *

When it comes to enlightening you and your family, just how far can a computer go?

* * * * *

The results are in—and they may well surprise you.

* * * * *

Where would you like to be in five years?

* * * * *

There are 50 things you can do to improve your health—but I'm only going to tell you 5 of them.

* * * * *

Don't read this letter unless you mean business.

* * * * *

I want you on my side.

* * * * *

What's your money doing while you're out there working?

* * * * *

I'd like to partner with you to help you achieve all your objectives.

* * * * *

The word "yo" has entered the dictionary. What next?

* * * * *

The check isn't in the mail—at least not yet.

* * * * *

Would you believe me if I promised to. . . ?

* * * * *

Old King Cole was a merry old soul. Of course, he didn't have to . . .

* * * * *

In business, it's give-and-take.

* * * * *

I'm going for it. Why don't you?

Here are some letters that don't grab the reader's attention effectively, plus their rewrites.

original:

We hope that our enthusiasm at the opportunity to serve you is apparent to you in the development of this proposal and in our recent

preachy

meetings. You should know that you would be an important and valued client to OPR and would be serviced as such. We would commit all of our resources toward helping your company achieve its objectives. **not believable**

rewrite:

Have we convinced you yet how enthusiastic we are to be working with you? We certainly hope so, because we do value your business and plan to give you the excellent service you deserve.

original:

Why would the reader care?

People are <u>constantly asking my opinion</u> about the future of interest

negative

rates for mortgages and home equity rates. <u>Unfortunately,</u> trying to predict whether rates will go up or down is next to impossible. But there is one thing that I am sure of.

a boring quote

<u>"Homeowners who have been thinking about borrowing money for any reason should seriously consider doing it now while interest rates are still low."</u>

rewrite:

Who knows where interest rates are going? I don't, and neither do you. And that's why now is the perfect time to borrow money—while mortgage rates are still so low.

original:

Dear Friend:

no "you" attitude

One of the "perks" of <u>my job as Director of The Craftsman Club</u> is being able to travel all over the country and to Europe to track down crafts books at their source. British publishers, for instance, offer an astonishing array. Unfortunately for crafters, however, many of these books never make it across the Atlantic.

So when I discover a stunning new book on hooked rugs from the British experts or the new nature crafts book by one of our favorite floral experts, I'm delighted. Because that is what we are all about:

Focus on your readers, not members.

<u>bringing our members the very best</u> books available on a wide variety of crafts, including many that are hard to find.

rewrite:

Dear Crafts Lover:

From New York to London and beyond, there's an astonishing array of crafts books you'd ordinarily never get a chance to see. I'd like to share these books with you by offering you a membership in our Craftsman Book Club.

Sound interesting? You might choose a stunning new book on hooked rugs—or perhaps the new nature crafts book by one of our favorite horticulture experts.

original:

But I *don't* know.   **Why repeat long words like *diversification*?**

As you know, diversification is a key investment principle to help you reach your long-term goals. But finding the most effective way to diversify isn't always easy. That's why I want to introduce you to Select Portfolios . . . offering a full level of diversification in one smart, easy investment.

Highlight specific benefits.

Not only diversified, but asset-allocated to help maximize potential return.

Diversification among the major asset classes, such as stocks, bonds,

Is this word necessary?

and cash investments, helps reduce the risk inherent in putting all your investments in one asset class. That's because different asset classes can perform differently under the same market conditions. For example, when stocks are doing well overall, bonds may not be.

rewrite:

You may already know that your best chance for making your investments work for you is by diversifying. That way, if stocks are doing well and bonds aren't, you're covered.

But have you ever heard of asset allocation? This sophisticated technique gives you an even better way to increase your possible return by delivering the right mix of stocks, bonds, and cash.

I'd like to explain how Select Portfolios can put asset allocation to work for you.

Openings to Avoid

In regard to your letter . . . [*say "concerning"*]

* * * * *

I have your letter at hand.

* * * * *

Per your communication . . .

* * * * *

Pursuant to your communication . . .

* * * * *

We have carefully investigated . . . [*better to give the results of the investigation*]

* * * * *

Attached (enclosed) please find . . .

* * * * *

This is to state . . .

* * * * *

I would like to take this opportunity . . .

* * * * *

It has come to my attention . . .

* * * * *

As you are well aware . . .

* * * * *

Thank you for your letter of May 1. [*better to thank the reader for some action taken in the letter*]

* * * * *

I have received your letter. . . .

* * * * *

The purpose of this letter is to . . .

* * * * *

Under separate cover please find . . .

* * * * *

It is our understanding that . . . [*say "We understand"*]

* * * * *

We are writing in response to . . . [*why not "We are pleased to answer"?*]

* * * * *

This will confirm . . .

I Is for *Interest*

Once you have your reader's attention, you need to focus on the merits of your product, service, or idea. You can do this by appealing to reason or emotion and benefits.

A company selling cellular service offers lifestyle benefits.

With cellular service, you're not tied to one place anymore. You have the freedom to stay in touch from almost anywhere—with friends, children, clients, colleagues—whoever is in your life. It means you can call for help if you have a flat tire . . . call to check for messages . . . call to say you'll be late for dinner. And you won't miss out on something important because someone can't get in touch with you.

A credit card discount company offers these benefits:

With your savings you can visit the same restaurants again and again, with no limit to how much you can save. And you can dine out more often. Our goal is simple: to give you a terrific selection of outstanding restaurants, from casual to formal—with cuisine that ranges from Thai to Cajun and French to good ol' American.

A promotion creates images for going Hawaiian:

Imagine yourself relaxing on the beach, gazing out at beautiful South Pacific vistas. . . . What are you waiting for? The land of pineapples, big waves, and some of the world's best beaches awaits you.

If you want a home equity loan, you'll gain these advantages by signing up with a particular company:

You can pay off your high-interest loans immediately, and could well end up paying hundreds of dollars less each month than you are paying now. Or, use the money for your big expenses—like home improvements, tuition, medical bills, or a new car. It could mean the difference between having a tight budget and having cash to spare.

The more specific the benefits, the greater the interest and appeal. Hence, the following credit card promotion boasts what the company calls "truly useful card member benefits."

You'll get 60-day price protection, extended warranty protection, and protection against loss, theft, breakage, and fire damage. You'll also enjoy quality 24-hour, toll-free customer service . . . free personalized convenience checks . . . instant cash at more than 200,000 ATMs worldwide . . . acceptance at more than 13 million locations . . . and more.

You can use these transitional phrases to move your reader along to your interest-raising advantages:

What does all this mean to you?

* * * * *

Here's why.

* * * * *

Don't just take my word for it.

* * * * *

And there's more!

* * * * *

Interested?

* * * * *

Sound like something you could use?

* * * * *

Want to learn more?

* * * * *

How can you benefit?

* * * * *

Better still . . .

* * * * *

What's in it for you?

* * * * *

Even more important . . .

* * * * *

Another benefit . . .

* * * * *

And what's really exciting about . . .

* * * * *

First of all, . . .

* * * * *

Along those lines, . . .

* * * * *

Just to update you . . .

* * * * *

Moving forward . . .

Besides showing advantages and benefits, you can offer guaranties, testimonials from happy customers, and free samples or trial periods. You can also offer a gift your customers can keep if they opt for a refund.

Price Issues

1. **Compare your prices favorably to the competition's.** If you're selling one encyclopedia volume for $59, you can mention that the most popular brand charges $100 for the same product.
2. **Sell bulk.** If you're selling an expensive cassette, note that it stretches out into "one-half mile of entertainment." Or your tires can become "20,000 miles of safe, comfortable driving."
3. **Make the parts more valuable than the whole.** Your makeup promotion costs $44, but if the parts were purchased separately, the cost would be $112.
4. **Hide the price.** You can promote a necklace as "three monthly credit card charges of $33 each" rather than stress the actual price of $99.

5

Motivate Your Reader to Act

The finest eloquence is that which gets things done.

—David Lloyd George,
British Prime Minister, 1916–1922

You have grabbed your reader's attention and have crafted compelling arguments. Now for the closer, which is almost as important as the opener.

Don't introduce new information in your ending. Instead, use your final paragraph to accomplish one or all of these goals:

1. Offer a suggestion on what action the readers should take.
2. Show how they will benefit from this action.
3. End on a cordial or positive note.

Remember the last part of the sales acronym.

M Is for *Motivation*

Stimuli to Action for Sales Letters

1. **Deadlines.** You can handwrite these or use a rubber stamp to draw attention to them. Or put them in an unusual position on the page.

2. **Discounts for quick action.** You might stress lower prices before a particular date and higher prices afterward.

3. **Limited availability.** The message is "hurry up and buy."

4. **Premiums.** Offer a special bonus for those who buy—a free book, for example.

5. **Contests, games, or sweepstakes.** Everyone likes to play, and deadlines get a fast response.

6. **Ease of response.** Make it easy for readers to act (provide a toll-free number or postage-paid envelope).

7. **Reminder of benefits.** Leave readers with an echo of the benefits you've already noted, using the same language.

SOME DOS AND DON'TS FOR ALL LETTERS

Don't

Overuse These Expressions

Do apologize, but not at the end. You want to leave your reader on a positive note.
I'm sorry.

* * * * *

robot talk
Thank you for the opportunity to be of service to you.

* * * * *

Try to give a date whenever possible.
At your convenience . . .

* * * * *

not forceful enough
If you would be so kind as to . . .

* * * * *

vague
I hope . . .

* * * * *

stuffy language
If you should have any questions . . .

* * * * *

weak
If it's not too much trouble . . .

Don't Use Participial Endings

The following endings are old-fashioned, vague, and incorrect grammatically:

Thanking you in advance.

* * * * *

Looking forward to hearing from you.

* * * * *

Hoping to hear from you.

Don't Thank People in Advance for Anything

Thanking in advance makes you sound out-of-date and impersonal, not cordial as some people mistakenly think.

weak:
Thank you in advance for your cooperation in this matter.

better:
Thank you for helping me with my problem. [*Yes, you're assuming the reader will help.*]

weak:

Thank you in advance for sending your check.

better:

Please send your check for $54 by May 3.

Don't
Use Clichés and Trite Expressions

Thank you for bringing this matter to my attention.

* * * * *

Thank you for your prompt attention to this matter.

* * * * *

If you have any further questions, do not hesitate to call. [*Also skip "feel free to call"*]

* * * * *

We look forward to serving you in the future.

* * * * *

We regret any inconvenience we may have caused you. [*Instead, talk about the frustration or problems you have caused the reader.*]

* * * * *

It has been a pleasure to be of assistance.

* * * * *

We appreciate your patronage.

* * * * *

We assure you that we will make every effort to provide optimal service to you in the future.

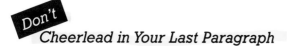

Cheerlead in Your Last Paragraph

Keep your thank-you short and to the point.

cheerleading:

Thank you so much for your contribution to our cause. Without your dedicated and enthusiastic response, we never would have reached our advantageous conclusion. Again, thank you.

better:

Thank you so much for your generous contribution. It has made a difference.

Invite People to Call With Questions

Many people ask readers to call with questions because they can't think of a better ending. If your reader has your phone number and would be perfectly comfortable calling you with questions, you can skip this phrase and end with your last factual point.

If you do solicit your reader to call, try rewording the request.

tired:

If you have any further questions, feel free to call.

better:

Please give me a call anytime if you have any questions. I'm always happy to hear from you.

better:

If there's anything else I can do for you, please be sure to call me at 555-9900.

Don't

Use Faddish Expressions That Sound Foolish

The one that comes immediately to mind is the silly *Your call is very important to us, so don't hang up.*

If the call is so important, don't keep people on hold forever, captive to your commercial messages or loud music. While this phrase is currently used for telephone communication, you get the picture. Think about the meaning of your words before trying them out on customers.

Don't

Use If When You Can Substitute a Stronger Word

weak:

> If it is convenient for you to see me, please call.

better:

> Please call to let me know when we can get together.

Don't

Wait for Your Customer to Call You

acceptable:

> Please call me to let me know a convenient time to meet.

better:

> I'll call you Tuesday morning to discuss when we can get together.

Do

Use Strong Language

Phrases like *Let's meet to discuss* or *Let's develop a plan* work well.

Words like *meet, decide, act, authorize,* and *recommend* (versus *it is recommended*) suggest power.

Do
End on a Positive Note Whenever Possible

instead of:

Again, we regret any inconvenience.

try:

Thank you for taking the time to write.

instead of:

We are sorry for your difficulty.

try:

We're going to make sure you receive the excellent service you de-serve from now on.

Do
Include a P.S. as a Stimulus to Action

good examples:

P.S. We have an idea that's too good for words. May we drop by to tell you about it?

* * * * *

P.S. If you decide by April 14, we have a special gift for you. Call and ask us about it.

* * * * *

P.S. Once you sign up, you'll be eating our mouth-watering steaks and chops for the same price you used to pay for chicken.

* * * * *

P.S. If you're ready to order now, choose the YES sticker. But if you're still undecided, the MAYBE sticker is your chance to sample our collection RISK FREE.

weak example:

> P.S. Remember, your satisfaction is always guaranteed. If at any time during the term of your subscription you decide to cancel, simply drop us a line and we'll send you a refund for all unmailed issues. You risk nothing, and the FREE gift is yours to keep.

> P.P.S. To get the best deal, subscribe for the longest term offered. By doing so, you will be protecting yourself from any price increase that might take place during the term of your subscription. Remember, our no-risk guarantee allows you to cancel at any time.

The P.S. is wordy, and the P.P.S. is always silly and unnecessary (overkill). The two segments above can be shortened into the following.

better:

> P.S. Your satisfaction is guaranteed. So if you ever decide to cancel, just drop us a line and we'll refund all unmailed issues. You risk nothing, and the FREE gift is yours to keep.

The place to "warn" your readers to protect themselves against possible price increases is in the sign-up area, where you push for a longer subscription term, not in the P.S.

Good Examples of General Closings

As soon as you send us your check, we'll immediately process it.

* * * * *

Thank you for telling us about your problem.

* * * * *

If there's anything I can do to help, please let me know.

* * * * *

Was I correct in thinking you would want to hear about my problem?

* * * * *

If you have any other questions, please give me a call.

* * * * *

I need your answer by January 2.

* * * * *

As soon as you pay this charge, we'll immediately reinstate your credit.

* * * * *

We believe this brochure will answer all your questions. But please call me at _____ if there's anything else you want to know.

* * * * *

Would you jeopardize your credit rating for so small an amount?

* * * * *

When can we get together to talk?

* * * * *

Any questions? Please give me a call anytime.

* * * * *

I'll give you a call soon. Meanwhile, we look forward to hearing from you anytime you have a question or need help.

* * * * *

Let's get together and talk about it. I'm confident that you'll find that our service will work for you.

* * * * *

I hope this information is helpful.

* * * * *

Thanks for your patience, Ms. Scott.

* * * * *

Thanks so much, Ms. Siegal, for the help you have given me up to now.

* * * * *

Please give us a chance to show you how our plan can turn things around for you.

* * * * *

We're proud to have you for a client. You know you'll get everything you need—and more—from us in the future.

* * * * *

We'll be ready to go into production within two months. I'm confident that you and your staff will be as excited as we are with the plans.

* * * * *

Before you make up your mind, please give me a chance to show you our "can do" attitude.

* * * * *

You asked us to do the impossible—and we did it. Thanks for giving us the chance.

* * * * *

Can you give me a few dates that would work for you?

* * * * *

Thanks so much for your confidence. It's going to be great working with you.

* * * * *

I'd like to discuss your needs in more detail. How about Monday, February 9? I'll call to confirm.

* * * * *

You can count on our full cooperation now and in all the months to come.

* * * * *

Barb, thanks so much for your understanding. Rest assured that this won't happen again.

* * * * *

Thanks so much for your consideration, Frank.

* * * * *

I'd appreciate hearing from you within the next week so that I can tell our manager what dates to hold for our meeting.

* * * * *

Let's keep working together toward a strong finish to an already strong year.

* * * * *

We need your check by June 12 to avoid having to take further action.

* * * * *

Please look over the enclosed brochure. Then either call me or drop me a note with your thoughts. I'll be waiting to hear from you.

* * * * *

You have nothing to lose—and much to gain—from taking us up on our offer today.

* * * * *

I'll call for an appointment next Tuesday to discuss how much time you'll save by installing E-mail at your site.

* * * * *

Which models would you like to try? Just check off your choice on our order blank.

* * * * *

Take a moment now to check off the items that interest you. We'll gladly send you a sample of each.

* * * * *

The coupon below will get you a copy with no obligation. Won't you mail it today?

* * * * *

We think you'll find our calling plan is exactly what you're looking for.

* * * * *

May we discuss your training needs with you? Just mail the enclosed card, and I'll call at a time you choose.

* * * * *

Act now and protect one of your most valuable assets—your health.

* * * * *

It all boils down to this: You can save at least 10% on your heating bills by signing up with us today.

* * * * *

Just give us a call if you have any questions.

* * * * *

Find out today how our service can help you. Just visit our office to discuss putting our staff to work for you.

* * * * *

You want to qualify for the discount. So be sure to complete the application and return it to us by April 3.

* * * * *

Won't you please complete the application and return it to us by March 3? That way you'll qualify for the discount.

* * * * *

Are you willing to give Jiffy Steaks a month's trial in your home at one-half the price? Your signature on the enclosed card will rush them on their way to you.

* * * * *

Mail your check today, and your order will be at your door within ten days.

* * * * *

Discover the savings. Just go over the enclosed price list. Then call us at 800-555-2222 to say, "I'd like to do business with YOU." You'll be glad you did.

* * * * *

How about it?

* * * * *

Take this important step now. I know you'll be delighted.

* * * * *

Don't let the competition get the edge on you.

* * * * *

Want to find out more? Call or fax us today.

* * * * *

Here's my suggestion. Try our steamer for a month. You can always return it if you're not delighted with your reduced dry-cleaning bills.

* * * * *

If this sounds like a great deal, you're right.

* * * * *

Give me a call anytime, or drop by my office. I'd be delighted to chat with you.

* * * * *

Don't hesitate— This deal's too good to miss.

* * * * *

Thirty thousand people like you have already ordered. Now you can, too.

6

Handle Account Management Issues With Sensitivity and Concern

Civility is not a sign of weakness, and sincerity is always subject to proof.

—*John Fitzgerald Kennedy*

There are three simple techniques for dealing with account management issues, sensitive or otherwise:

1. Be personal.
2. Sound conversational.
3. Act sincere.

Apologies

Typically, we see the following kind of apology. It's cold and filled with self-serving clichés.

> We apologize for the unsatisfactory service you have experienced with Allied Corp. The problem you encountered is not a typical situation experienced by our customers, but we are updating our operating procedures so that you will not encounter similar problems in the future. We want to assure you that we will make every effort to provide optimal service in the future.
>
> Thank you for the opportunity to serve you.

Substitute a more personal, conversational, and sincere choice of language.

improved:

> I'm so sorry you've had an unpleasant experience with our service. I've already spoken with Sara Jacoby in our billing department about why your last two payments were never posted. It turns out that we have another customer with your name, and you can guess what happened. While this is a rare problem, it still shouldn't have happened.
>
> You'll be pleased to know we have cleared up the confusion and your future payments will be credited to your account.
>
> Thanks for being patient with us, Mr. Lawrence.

Thank-You's

Suppose you're happy to have some new business. Why not write a gracious note to the person who helped you get it?

gracious:

> It's an understatement to say how delighted I am to have won your account. Thank you for the part you played in this process. I promise to do everything to justify your confidence.

Here's a wordy letter to a customer discussing some service offered. The writer mistakenly thinks that the more language she offers, the more sincere she sounds.

wordy:

> Dear Jonathan:
>
> On behalf of all your Triptex associates, I take this opportunity to thank you for your support and understanding and, most importantly, for having provided us with enough details to help us in solving the complex set of problems we have been experiencing with your product these past few weeks.
>
> As you already know, we have addressed a multiple set of problems that have been impacting you and your users. Below is an explanation of the steps we have taken in order to resolve the issues you have already raised as well as the steps we'll be taking to prevent this from happening in the future.

Use spell check!

I will preface by stating that Monday will be the proof <u>wether</u> we have really addressed these problems, and you will be our best judge.

Again, careless!

Again, I thank you for <u>you</u> understanding, patience, and the opportunity you have given us to correct our problems as well as to continue to be your service provider.

Besides the bad spelling and wordiness, there's another problem in this letter. It doesn't start with a statement of purpose.

Each time we pick up a letter, we ask, "Why are you bothering me?" You should answer that question right up front with your opening, as in this rewrite of the previous letter.

purpose stated up front:

Dear Jonathan:

I'd like to explain what we've done to correct the problems that have been troubling you and your users. Thanks for giving us all the details and for being so supportive and understanding. I've listed the steps we've taken below. Monday will be the test as to whether our efforts have succeeded. Meantime, we're working hard to give you the excellent service you deserve—and we appreciate your patience.

Request for Information

Here are two versions of a written request for information.

original:

impersonal opening

Thank you for your request for information about our investment funds. The material that you have requested has been sent out by our Customer Service department, and I hope it is of help to you.

If you should have any questions, please contact our Financial Services number at 800-555-1111. <u>A representative will be happy to assist you.</u>   **sounds like a recording**

Allied appreciates your interest and looks forward to serving you in the future.

While the difference between a "good" and a "bad" letter is largely subjective, wouldn't you respond more favorably to this version of the same letter?

rewrite:

I'm pleased to respond to your request for information about our funds. Our Customer Service department has already sent our prospectus to you. I hope that this material answers all your questions.

If you would like any other information, please call our Financial Services line at 800-555-1111. A representative will be glad to help.

Welcome to Allied, Ms. Brill. We're looking forward to doing business with you.

Good Response to a Customer

Here's an example of a good letter a company sent to a customer who offered a suggestion.

I'm pleased to reply to your letter of October 24, suggesting that we supply return labels with our orders. Your idea is an excellent one. I've passed it on to our manager for possible action.

Thanks for taking the time to write, Ms. Hall. We're always grateful when our customers help us make our service even better.

Answering Complaints

Here are some guidelines for defusing anger and reestablishing goodwill.

1. **Apologize and acknowledge the customer's frustration. This doesn't mean you're accepting blame.** Use phrases like these:

This must have been disappointing for you.

* * * * *

I agree. A tire ordinarily should last longer than two years.

* * * * *

I can see this is frustrating for you. It is for me, too.

2. **Identify problems by name so your message doesn't sound like a form letter.**

   weak:

   Thank you for informing us of your problem with our merchandise.

   better:

   Thank you for telling us about the mistake we made with your sweater shipment.

3. **Correct the problem quickly and fairly.** Of course, you do have to decide whether the customer's business is worth the adjustment you may have to make.

   If everything you have offered still won't satisfy your customer, you may have to respond this way:

   I'm sorry you aren't happy with our service. We believe we have done everything we could to get your order to you on time.

   Obviously, though, we didn't meet your expectations, and we're sorry for that.

   We'll miss working with you, Ms. Bennett.

4. **Stress concrete action you'll take.**

   weak:

   We're taking precautions to keep this from happening again.

   better:

   We are putting a note on your account to make sure you won't be double-billed again.

5. **Be believable in your promises.**

weak:

> We're going to hold a seminar for all our customer service reps to alert them to the importance of courtesy.

better:

> I'm going to have Mr. Charon's supervisor speak to him about his behavior toward you.

weak:

> We're referring your letter to the appropriate party for resolution.

better:

> I'm giving your letter to Phyllis Quinn, our customer service manager. She'll call you next week to discuss how to resolve your problem.

6. **Keep your promises.** Follow up if you're delayed in keeping to a promised date.

7. **Use positive or consoling phrases.** For example:

> Let me find out for you.

* * * * *

> There seems to be some confusion about . . .

* * * * *

> You're right to be concerned.

* * * * *

> We share your concern.

* * * * *

> I can understand your frustration.

* * * * *

There's no excuse for . . .

$$* * * * *$$

I agree with you that . . .

8. **Offer something extra.**

   - Make a phone call for the customer.
   - Hand deliver documents.
   - Give a discount on future business.

9. **Be gracious in accepting criticism.** Use a phrase such as *It's a big help to hear from customers when things aren't quite as expected.*

SAMPLE ACCOUNT MANAGEMENT LETTER SEGMENTS

good approach:

You're right. We do promise two-day turnaround. I'm going to take care of this problem myself. Here's what I'm planning to do for you.

good letter:

I wish I could complete your order for ten sofa covers. Unfortunately, this type of cover doesn't come in the size you requested, and we aren't able to custom-cut them.

What I can suggest is that you call Abel's in Springfield. They have a large custom department. I hope this works out for you, Ms. Molesworth.

Response to a Problem

weak:

Dear Mr. Grunewald:

I want you to know that we sincerely regret your recent experience in regard to your purchase of Papa's Popcorn. We are gratified that you took the time out of your busy schedule to inform us of your feelings. It is only through customers like <u>yourself</u> that we can improve our service.   **Grammar mistake—should be *you.***

We assure you that we have investigated this matter and have learned that the shipment to your area was indeed backdated. That is why you <u>perceived</u> it as stale.
Sounds as if staleness is only in the reader's mind.

Under separate cover, we are taking the liberty of sending you a case of Papa's Popcorn. <u>We appreciate your patronage</u> and apologize for any inconvenience.   **stuffy language**

improved:

Dear Mr. Grunewald:

I was very sorry to learn of your recent unpleasant experience with our popcorn. You're right to expect better service from our products.

There's no excuse for a stale shipment going to your area, so I won't even try to offer you one. Instead, I'm sending you a fresh case of Papa's Popcorn—with our hope that this will make up for at least a part of your frustration.

Thanks for writing, Mr. Grunewald.

P.S. If you don't receive the popcorn by April 4, please give me a call at 201-555-4253.

Pleasant Response to a Complaint

I'm so sorry that you felt you were treated rudely at Merkham's. I have discussed your complaint with Grace O'Hara, and she has assured me that she is deeply sorry for having upset you.

Please use the enclosed discount coupon the next time you're in the store to make your shopping with us even more enjoyable.

Good Response From an Airline to a Customer Complaint

You're certainly correct to think we would want to hear about your problem. And here's what we've done about it.

First, we're sharing your complaint with Ms. Baker's supervisor, Rick Mallone, who will ask her for her side of the issue. Also, we'll put a copy of your letter in Ms. Baker's file. We use these files for long-term evaluation.

There's no excuse for you to receive less than perfect service on any of our flights. Will you give us another chance?

Good Account Management Letter

You're certainly right to share with us in your letter of July 21 your frustration concerning your order delays. Since we know how important it is to avoid keeping you waiting, we talk extensively with our suppliers to plan our own orders carefully—just so you're not put in this position.

Sometimes, despite our best efforts, things just don't work out. And we're sincerely sorry for this. I'd prefer to be able to tell you we have your merchandise. But since I can't do that right now, I'll follow your instructions and remove you from our mailing list.

I only hope you'll reconsider and give us another chance to provide the items and service that will make you a happy customer again.

nice tone:

You were right to let us know about the disappointment you had with our skis. We don't want you to have anything from Blackwell's that isn't completely satisfactory.

Good Apology for Poor Billing Practices

As you have correctly guessed, our computers are to blame for all the nagging payment reminders we've been sending. I'm really sorry they have been such a nuisance.

Unfortunately, I can't be sure you won't receive another notice. But your letter did stimulate me to discuss our problem with Nadia Gorchek, our chief troubleshooter. She has promised to keep an eye on your account until our systems are running better. Meanwhile, please excuse us, and please just ignore any more of the form reminders.

Thanks for being an excellent customer and for being so patient with us.

Good Response to a Complaint

You have rightly complained about our telemarketing techniques. Unfortunately, we've made some mistakes, like the excessive number of calls you mentioned in your recent letter.

From now on, we're using a computer program to make sure we won't bother you with more than one call. Thanks to you and other considerate customers, we're learning how to offer you the excellent service you deserve.

Good Apology for Poor Service

I'm sorry we blundered on your sweater order. Our staff has been with us for many years, but once in a while they slip up. Unfortunately, someone wasn't paying careful attention when you placed your order. And there's no excuse for that.

You should receive the right sweaters within a week. My direct line is 855-9900. Please give me a call if you have any concerns about your future orders.

We do value your business, Ms. Claire, and appreciate your patience with us.

Good Explanation of a Service Charge

Thank you for your letter of March 18, explaining your concern about our service charge of $18.

Of course you're correct in pointing out that you almost always pay your bill on time, and it's certainly unpleasant to pay a charge for one slipup. Our billing is computerized, however, and machines have trouble distinguishing between excellent customers like you and those who repeatedly delay paying.

I'm pleased to remove this charge as you have requested. Please note my personal phone number above. If you have any other problems, I'll be happy to help.

Polite Way of Standing Firm on Your Bill

We certainly agree with you that it's unpleasant to live without a working refrigerator. That's why we dispatched a service rep right away to find out what went wrong.

His report shows that the outlet into which your refrigerator was plugged was overloaded. This caused a short circuit and a resulting loss of power. You'll see in your handbook some points about power requirements.

It's unfortunate that you lost all the food, and I'm sorry our repair department didn't explain clearly what caused the trouble.

We're pleased that everything is working now and that the refrigerator was not to blame. Since the problem does not lie with our equipment, we'd appreciate receiving payment of our bill by November 12, 1997.

Denial of a Credit Request

poor:

Thank you for your letter inquiring about a Miller's charge account.

negative

At the present time, <u>we do not offer a charge account.</u> The methods of payment we accept are checks, money orders, and major credit cards.

Should be "you," not "yourself."

We are very appreciative of customers like <u>yourself</u> who care enough about Miller's to take the time to write to us. We hope you will remain a happy, interested customer for many years to come. Whenever we can be of service, <u>please do not hesitate</u> to contact us.

typical cliché ending

improved:

I appreciate your recent letter asking us for a Miller's charge account. I wish we could say yes to your request, but right now we only accept checks, money orders, and major credit cards.

You may have noticed that all large mail-order companies require payment on purchase. There's actually a good reason for this policy. So many thousands of orders go out each day that billing customers would be hard—and would also make our products more expensive.

If there's anything else I can do for you, please let me know. Thanks for taking the time to write.

Explanation of a Shipping Charge

poor:

Thank you for giving us your input concerning the $3.50 shipping charge that we instituted in the spring of 1995. We value our

Value *this* reader's opinion, not all your customers'.

customers' opinions and appreciate knowing how this decision affects you.

The shipping charge decision was one of the most difficult decisions we had to face. We certainly recognize and understand how impor-

Again, address *this* reader's needs and interests.

tant our free shipping policy was to many of our customers and were proud of the fact that we were the only major mail-order company to provide it. It was a tradition with Golds for over 60 years.

Ultimately, the decision had to be made in the best interests of Golds and our future customers. In 1994, shipping expenses were more than $40 million. It is simply more and more unrealistic, in today's business environment, to continue to absorb our outbound shipping costs if

very "we" oriented

we are to maintain competitive pricing and enhance services to our customers in the coming years.

Our commitments to you now and in the future will be to offer one of the lowest, most competitive shipping charges in the industry and to provide the best in both personal services and quality products designed to meet your needs. We sincerely hope that you understand why this change is necessary for us and that you will continue to be a Golds customer.

improved:

Thank you for your input on the $3.50 shipping charge we have recently instituted. We value your opinion and appreciate hearing how this change affects you.

We wish we could have continued our free shipping policy, a tradition we enjoyed for over 60 years. But when our shipping costs rose to over $40 million in 1994, it became a matter of simple economics. Only by adding the charge could we stay competitive in our overall prices. We were the last of the major mail-order companies to hold out for no shipping fee. And like you, we miss the good old days.

We're pleased to promise you that we're committed to keeping our shipping charge one of the lowest in the industry—and to offering you the excellent service and quality you deserve.

Collecting Money

Years ago, an intimidating letter like this would easily inspire payment.

If you do not remit the full amount of your liability within 30 days, we shall be forced to take legal action against you.

Today, appeals to fairness or to friendship work better than intimidation in the first or even the second collection letter. Of course, if being nice doesn't work, you may still have to resort to threats.

Appeal to Fairness

Let's look at the record. We were fair with you and sent you your merchandise on time and in excellent condition.

Won't you be fair with us in return and send us your check for $150 today?

Appeal to Friendship

Do you have a problem we can help you with? Is there some reason you haven't paid your bill?

Please call me collect so we can discuss an amicable way to settle your account.

Your customer may just have a reason for not paying. You're willing to set up a payment schedule or do whatever it takes as long as you know you'll ultimately be paid.

Reminder Note

You may want to start the collection process with a friendly reminder or a note suggesting that the customer may have forgotten to pay.

> Just a friendly reminder of our terms, which are full payment by the 28th of the month.

> Our account will be off your mind if you send your payment for $78 in the enclosed envelope. And you'll avoid a finance charge if you mail it today.

Assuming the Reader Forgot

> Maybe you've forgotten—

> Possibly you've overlooked our bill—

> In any event, you still owe us $100 from our last bill. Why not send the minimum payment of $25 by June 4 to avoid a finance charge? We'll both be glad you did.

Concern About the Customer's Credit

> In business, we all understand the importance of a good credit reputation. That's why we were concerned when you jeopardized your rating by not paying the $240 you owe us.

> We'd like to avoid reporting your past-due account to the local credit bureau. Won't you pay us today so that we can all rest more easily about your rating?

Final Collection Letter

> First we reminded you, and then we urged you. Unfortunately, there's only one alternative left. Since you have not replied to our earlier

past-due notices, we're ready to place your account in our attorney's hands.

For you, there is still one alternative: Send us your payment of $134 by May 8. Otherwise, we'll be forced to take an action which, frankly, we'd prefer to avoid.

a strong appeal:

We care about your credit rating.

And that's one reason we're trying not to turn your account over to our attorney for collection. Also, lawyers are expensive—both for us and for you.

Sending us your check for $80 within the next seven days will avoid the unpleasant action we're both not going to like.

It's in your hands now. We're counting on you to do the right thing.

Here are two old, but still highly effective collection letters.

appeal to humor:

Dear Ms. Chen:

Would you please send me the name of a good lawyer in your area? We're planning to sue you for nonpayment of your bill.

a subtle threat:

Dear Mr. Davies:

You will sleep a lot better in your home tonight if you pay us today. [*This letter received an 83 percent return.*]

**The assumption is he won't sleep at home anymore
if he doesn't pay—he'll be in jail.**

Dunning Notice

weak:

impersonal opening

We requested a past-due payment on our last monthly statement to you. To date, we have not received payment. Please send your payment to us as soon as possible to ensure continued employee coverage.

Our records show your group account is currently paid to September 1, 1995. <u>If we do not</u> hear from you by October 9, 1995, we will <u>no</u>

negative language

<u>longer be able</u> to continue your group coverage. Claims for services your employees received after September 1, 1995, will not be paid.

stuffy approach

We value your business and appreciate your prompt attention to this matter. Please note that if we cancel your coverage and you wish to apply for reinstatement, your application will be subject to a minimum 90-day waiting period and the approval of our underwriters.

If you have any questions or have already submitted the overdue payment(s), please contact us at the phone number above.

improved:

WE NEED YOUR HELP.

Is there some reason you haven't responded to our past-due notice on your last month's statement? Please call me if there's a problem we can help you with. Otherwise, we'll need your payment of $550 by October 9, 1995, to avoid these potential penalties if we cancel your account:

1. You would be subject to a 90-day waiting period before we could reinstate you.
2. Your reinstatement would be subject to our underwriters' approval.
3. Claims for services your employees received after September 1, 1995, would not be paid.

If you have any questions or have already paid your bill, please call me at the number above.

Date to Remember

To avoid cancellation, we need you to send your payment or call us by October 9, 1995.

7

Use Graphics, Gadgets, and Gimmicks as Highlighting Tools

Written reports stifle creativity.

—H. Ross Perot

We began experimenting with the standard letter format in the 1970s. Today, sales letter design possibilities are limited only by the boundaries of your imagination. There are, however, some established techniques that may work for you, especially when you're writing to masses of people you don't know. If you're writing an account management letter, on the other hand, avoid using any language that sounds too much like a pitch.

THE HEADLINE

Because it's the first part of the letter that the reader sees, the headline helps decide whether you will be read or rejected. It's used to grab and stimulate interest.

Points to Consider

1. Don't use this important area to summarize the offer or give away too many details.
2. Do keep the headline short—a few lines at most.
3. Do try handwriting an overline (or printing it so that it looks handwritten) to personalize it.

much too long:

THERE ARE 22 IMPORTANT THINGS THAT YOU SHOULD KNOW BEFORE YOU RE-
TIRE—ABOUT PENSION PLANS, SOCIAL SECURITY, TAX CHANGES, AND INVESTMENT
CHANGES. THEY'RE ALL EXPLAINED IN OUR NO-NONSENSE FINANCIAL GUIDE. SEND
FOR YOUR FREE COPY TODAY.

improved:

TWENTY-TWO IMPORTANT THINGS YOU SHOULD KNOW BEFORE YOU RETIRE

effect spoiled through poor language choice:

ACQUIRE THE EATER'S CLUB CARD AND RECEIVE 10,000 FREQUENT FLYER MILES
ON ANY MAJOR U.S. AIRLINE.

better:

GET THE EATER'S CLUB CARD—AND EARN 10,000 FREQUENT FLYER MILES ON
ANY MAJOR U.S. AIRLINE.

Here's a handwritten headline responding to a request for information on mutual funds—in large letters to add a little drama.

Thanks!

And you're welcome!

Thanks for asking for our pamphlet describing how our mutual funds
can be put to work for you.

And you're welcome to join our growing family of investors who have
placed their confidence in us—to the tune of $3.4 billion.

Other headlines are more traditional.

ATTENTION:
A NEW WAY TO SAVE . . .

* * * * *

JUST MAIL BACK THE CERTIFICATE BELOW TO PUT AN EXTRA $50 IN YOUR POCKET.

* * * * *

LET ME SHOW YOU HOW YOU CAN SAVE MONEY ON YOUR HEATING BILLS . . . MORE THAN YOU'D GUESS.

* * * * *

SPEND $50 DINING OUT EACH
WEEK. . . . IN ONE YEAR YOU'LL
SAVE $520!

* * * * *

PLEASE HURRY

* * * * *

IT'S NOT TOO LATE TO TAKE ADVANTAGE OF TODAY'S LOW RATES!

* * * * *

DEAR TAXPAYER:

HELP!!!

IF YOU'RE LIKE ME, YOU'RE CRYING OUT FOR HELP IN KEEPING YOUR TAX-PAYING HEAD ABOVE WATER.

Words That Work in Headlines

new	best	confidential	guaranteed	save
help	start	stop	fast	don't
value	free	announcing	improved	latest
now	discover	important	approved	instant

SUBHEADINGS

Subheadings break up the text and help guide the reader through the document.

> *Now you can claim a Pennysaver Card with a credit line of $5,125. Just fill out and mail back the acceptance certificate below. It's that easy.*
>
> YOU PAY NO ANNUAL FEE!
>
> *Your preapproved Pennysaver Card has no annual fee. So you can enjoy the convenience of buying what you want, at any time.*

It's also common to see a number of headings placed in the left margin.

20% savings every time ⎯⎯⎯⎯⎯⎯⎯⎯⎯⎯⎯⎯⎯⎯⎯⎯⎯⎯

⎯⎯⎯⎯⎯⎯⎯⎯⎯⎯⎯⎯⎯⎯⎯⎯⎯⎯

no limits ⎯⎯⎯⎯⎯⎯⎯⎯⎯⎯⎯⎯⎯⎯⎯⎯⎯⎯⎯⎯

⎯⎯⎯⎯⎯⎯⎯⎯⎯⎯⎯⎯⎯⎯⎯⎯⎯⎯

over 6,000 restaurants ⎯⎯⎯⎯⎯⎯⎯⎯⎯⎯⎯⎯⎯⎯⎯⎯⎯⎯

⎯⎯⎯⎯⎯⎯⎯⎯⎯⎯⎯⎯⎯⎯⎯⎯⎯⎯

and more . . . ⎯⎯⎯⎯⎯⎯⎯⎯⎯⎯⎯⎯⎯⎯⎯⎯⎯⎯⎯⎯

⎯⎯⎯⎯⎯⎯⎯⎯⎯⎯⎯⎯⎯⎯⎯⎯⎯⎯

THE JOHNSON BOX

The Johnson Box is a typed legend placed above the salutation and set off with a border of stars.

too much of the message:

* *

For generations, *Newsline* has provided readers like you with a panorama of contemporary America.

Today, *Newsline* maintains its proud tradition as America's favorite coffee table magazine. It entertains, amuses, and enlightens while providing you with important medical and financial information.

Find out for yourself RISK-FREE. Let us send you the latest issue of *Newsline* to sample at absolutely no cost or obligation to you.

What's more, if you like what you see, we'll send you a FREE GIFT, too! Please read on.

* *

Instead of being provocative, the box above is weighed down by the depth of the message.

better—everyone loves a quiz:

* *

TRUE OR FALSE	TRUE	FALSE
1. It's much harder to keep weight off than it is to lose it.	____	____
2. There's no diet invented that will help you lose weight without going hungry.	____	____
3. You can't lose weight unless you exercise too.	____	____
4. Everything you love to eat is fattening and bad for you.	____	____

* *

RUBBER STAMPS

Often slanted for visual emphasis, messages stamped on the letter (or that seem to be stamped—they're really printed) suggest a personal quality. They are short and catchy.

The following is a technique growing in popularity. It's a personal note—either handwritten or printed to look handwritten—attached to the letter.

> *Give us a minute of your time, Ms. Brill.*
> *I think you'll like what you see!*

Another kind of note has created a lot of interest lately. How would you react if you received a clipping about a product with this handwritten note pasted on it?

> *John—*
> *Thought this might interest you.*
> *L.*

You might well think long and hard about which "L" sent this to you—and even ask around the office, which would give the note more exposure.

The problem with this kind of ploy is that as soon as people catch on, it quickly outlives its usefulness. And then it's on to the next short-lived gimmick!

HIGHLIGHTING

The benefit of using color (often yellow, pink, or blue overlays), bolding, or underlining is obvious—the eye goes right to the language you've chosen to highlight.

On the other hand, the reader tends to ignore the rest of the letter, which can be a drawback if you have a lot to say.

INVERTED WRITING

The dark background with white lettering is a dramatic effect.

> YOU'RE PREAPPROVED FOR THIS
> EXCEPTIONAL VISA CARD.

ONE-SENTENCE QUESTIONS

Increasingly popular in capturing attention, one-sentence questions create interest as shown in the underlined portions of the following letter.

We're pleased to answer your recent inquiry and pinpoint some advantages of signing with our service.

First of all, you'll be able to coordinate your activities with greater accuracy and speed (at least 20 percent faster) than ever before. Also, your field personnel will exchange information easily, retrieve or submit information to databases, and collect E-mail—all while out of the office.

Sound like a service you could use?

A growing number of companies can offer you portable terminals and applications software. Still, our network technology is an open global standard. Its users avoid the limitations of proprietary chips, codes, or software and benefit from competitive pricing.

Interested?

GRAPHIC MARKS

Here is a sample of some of the graphic tools you can use to highlight and separate ideas.

bullet   •
solid, hollow, or shaded box   ■   □   ❐
inverse bullet   ▣
square diamond   ❖
triangle right   ▶
triangle left   ◀
solid arrow   →
checkmark   √
boxed words | *message* |
diamond   ◇
lines made of asterisks   *******************

8

Get Started Quickly by Planning Memos and Reports

Every moment spent planning saves three or four in execution.

—*Crawford Greenwalt, President, Du Pont*

Few of us can organize our thoughts effectively without some kind of plan—even one that's jotted down on a scrap of paper.

Planning before you write achieves these benefits:

1. You'll eliminate at least 25 percent of unnecessary language.
2. Your documents will have a much better chance of making sense.
3. You'll state your purpose up front.
4. You'll organize your thoughts so they flow logically.

When you write off the top of your head, you're likely to write in a narrative, "once upon a time" style. This is how we were taught to write as children, and is what is known as the standard pyramid design—our weakest way of organizing thoughts.

Your English teacher probably encouraged you to write in this style as you discussed your reaction to a particular novel or other piece of literature. However, few readers today have the luxury of sifting through a lot of background details to finally reach the main point. Time is simply too limited, as is our attention span.

Standard Pyramid

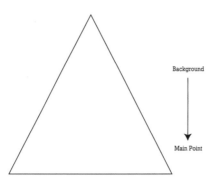

The problem with this approach is that there is a strong possibility you'll lose your reader in a mass of background details before the main point is ever reached.

Lately, we're borrowing a design that newspapers have been relying on for years. It is known as an inverted pyramid design.

Inverted Pyramid

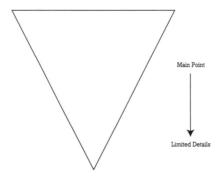

Beginning with your main point (often your purpose for writing) helps you to eliminate unnecessary background details. You certainly grab your reader's attention more effectively.

Your plan always depends on what you're trying to accomplish. For example, if you want your readers to *remember* an action, discuss it as close as possible to the end of the page (we remember the last thing we read better than any other part of the document).

On the other hand, if you want to *persuade* readers to accept your point of view, start out by telling them what you want. Then tell them all over again at the end of the document. Also, if there are five actions you want them to take, be sure to list the most important one first, where it will have the greatest emphasis.

There are several formulas and designs aimed at getting you started quickly and helping you organize your thoughts. The newest, mind-mapping, is now being used in grade schools to help young students map out their thoughts.

Mind-mapping is an excellent planning technique, and it helps you get to the point quickly. Draw a circle in the center of your page and within it write the main point you're trying to express—in the form of a complete sentence.

Then develop your points and subpoints in circles branching out from your central circle. Use verbs as much as you can in your secondary circles.

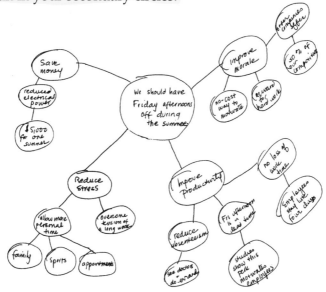

Any thought process is more logical when we map it out before we write.

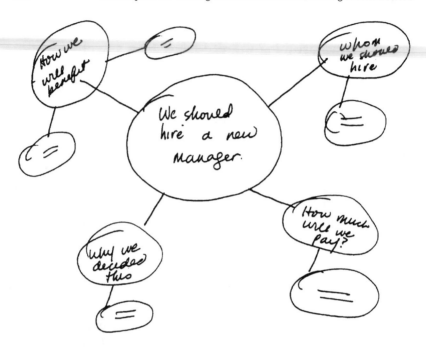

The trick to making this technique work for you is to follow the map as you write.

REPORTS AND MEMOS

While letters rely heavily on tone and warmth to create appeal, reports and memos (including E-mail) are less concerned with being friendly than with quick, clear transmittal of information.

Here are some formulas to help you get started quickly and organize effectively. Each is meant to accomplish a particular purpose—as opposed to mind-mapping, which can be used for any kind of writing or purpose.

When You're Writing About a Problem

Use the P-A-S formula.

P	is for *problem* statement
A	is for *analysis* of problem
S	is for *solution*

weak: narrative opening

Quite some time ago, we established a policy of minimum order multiples on basic stock merchandise. This policy was originally set up to speed up the processing of orders in Deer Park and to force the marketing department to identify slow-moving shades. If you are only ordering one or two of a shade, should you really clog up your stock with an item that sells so slowly?

I know from speaking with many of you that we are all concerned with the large number of slow-moving items in our line. I have stated in our policy below what is to be adhered to, and I hope you will comply, since it's the easiest way for our company to get rid of our slow movers.

The minimum quantities are listed on each basic stock order form next to the item number. All color merchandise that indicates a minimum order of three should be interpreted as three per shade.

hard to follow

If we outline this memo according to the P-A-S formula, rewriting it is a lot easier and a lot more coherent.

P	"Stock is moving slowly because our sales force doesn't follow our policy."
A	"We instituted the policy to speed up orders and identify slow-moving stock."
S	Direct staff to follow guidelines.

rewrite:

We have a problem with slow-moving stock because our sales force isn't following our minimum shade order policy.

We instituted this policy to speed up order processing in Deer Park and to ensure that marketing identifies slow-moving shades.

ACTION NEEDED

Please ask your staff to follow the minimum order guidelines on each basic stock order form next to the item number.

Note: When color merchandise says "minimum of three," this means three per shade.

When You're Writing to Persuade

In the problem memo, you end with the action you want taken because you want it remembered. When you're writing to persuade, you begin with what you want and repeat this at the end of the document.

When you're writing to persuade, the P-R-E-P formula can work for you.

P   is for *point of view* or opinion
R   is for *reasons* you hold this point of view
E   is for *examples* to support your reasons
P   is for *point of view* restated, plus any action

The P-R-E-P formula can translate your story line into a logical pyramid, as follows:

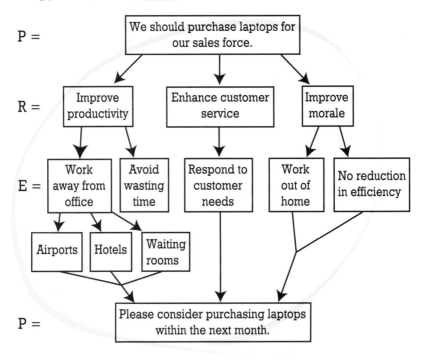

Once you have the outline squared away, the memo more or less writes itself.

We should purchase laptops for all members of our sales force for the following reasons:

Improve productivity:
Laptops will allow our staff to work more efficiently when they are away from the office. They can use time productively when in airports, hotels, waiting rooms, etc.

Enhance customer service:
Right now, we're out of the office 30% of the time. When issues arise, we can respond faster to our customers.

Improve morale:
Through the use of this equipment, we'll all have a chance to work out of our homes more with no reduction in efficiency.

I've included a cost breakdown for your review. Please consider purchasing laptops for all sales associates within the next month.

When You're Writing Simply to Inform

1. Begin with a statement of your purpose for writing.
2. Give the factual details (*who, what, when, where, why,* and *how*), using headings to distinguish between categories of thought.
3. End with an action statement or a brief personal comment. Keep your thank-you short. And don't request your reader to call you with any questions unless you provide a phone extension. Don't even include a closing statement if none is needed. Just end with your best factual point.

original: **The reader isn't sure of this opener's purpose.**

Agency trading involves executing orders for customers without taking security positions of your own. Profit is made from the spread between the purchase and sale rather than fluctuations in prices of positions held. In addition, we must charge a customer commission in order to cover the costs of buying the shares in the local market, such as commissions and exchange fees. Operational costs and overhead must also be considered.

By now, the reader is tired.

The market price at which the trade is executed is known as the gross price. When commission is added (or subtracted), it becomes the net price. The total funds after commission are known as the net proceeds.

If a customer wishes to purchase shares, we must first purchase the shares, unless we hold a position in that particular security. When a salesperson is buying or selling shares for a customer, he will make a profit, not in the difference between the buy and sell price, but by charging a credit. There are various forms of credit that a salesperson can charge in different situations.

The four types of credit are Standard, Special, Flat, and Additional. Each type can be used in different situations, depending on what is worked out between the salesperson and trader. Both parties must be aware of the credit being used when booking a trade. If the credit is not booked in the same fashion on both sides, the net proceeds will not match, even though the net prices may.

The headings in the rewrite of the previous memo make a big difference in readability.

rewrite:

Here is an overview of Agency Trading.

DESCRIPTION OF TRADING

You execute customers' orders without taking your own security positions. Profit comes from the spread between purchase and sale (not from fluctuating prices in held positions).

We charge commission to cover the costs of buying shares in the local market (e.g., commissions and exchange fees, operating costs, and overhead).

PRICING TERMS

Gross price: This is the market price at which the trade is executed.

Net price: This is the price when commission is added or subtracted.

Net proceeds: These are the total funds after commission.

PURCHASING DETAILS

When a customer wants to purchase shares through us, we purchase them—unless we hold a position in the security. The salesperson makes a profit by charging a credit, not because of a difference between buying and selling price.

FOUR CREDIT TYPES: STANDARD, SPECIAL, FLAT, AND ADDITIONAL

Each type can be used, depending on what the salesperson and the trader work out.

Both parties must know which credit is used when booking a trade. If the credit is not booked the same way, the net proceeds won't match even if the prices match.

Besides allowing the reader to skim, the rewrite above provides the ability to find what's of interest and ignore the rest. Your busy manager will be particularly thankful for this timesaver.

The second version of the following letter provides another example of how headings and graphic aids can improve the efficiency of your internal documents.

original:

Hickory entered into exclusive distribution agreements with Express Products (EP) to distribute the Lanewalker and Excel. EP, in business since 1954, is owned and operated by Michael Black. EP is principally a distributor of products to the bowling industry, including maintenance and cleaning machines, lane conditioners and cleaners, and other equipment. EP's distribution network is worldwide, including all 50 states and 35 foreign countries. EP's customers are mainly distributors. However, it does sell to military lanes and some bowling centers.

rewrite:

Hickory entered into exclusive distribution agreements with Express Products, Inc. (EP) to distribute the Lanewalker and Excel.

EP DETAILS

- In business since 1954, EP is owned and operated by Michael Black.
- Principally, it distributes products to the bowling industry (e.g., maintenance and cleaning machines, lane conditioners and cleaners, and other equipment).
- Its distribution network includes all 50 states and 35 foreign nations.
- While its customers are primarily distributors, it does sell to military lanes and some bowling centers.

When you're writing to busy managers, you should label everything you write to save time and identify subjects. A good label provides clues to the reader as to what is to come.

Examples of Labels

Background	Criteria	Definition	Findings
Examples	Recommendation	Problems	Costs
Solution	Actions to take	Advantages	Alternatives
Disadvantages	Options	Benefits	Next steps

You can also highlight information by using the word *note* as a label, as in the following example.

Note: Please remember to bring the Intell papers to the meeting on Tuesday.

If you find yourself writing the same types of documents over time, you may want to create your own template, as in the accompanying example. All you have to do is fill in the spaces each time you have to write a report.

CALL REPORT

Name   Date
Address   Call/Meeting

Phone   Distribution

Fax

Attending

Purpose of Call

Details of Discussion

Follow-Up

Date of Next Call

A combination of vertical and horizontal headings can work well, as in this example.

To generate interest in the new LAUNDEX detergent promotion, we have initiated a sales contest with the following features:

Broker groups:	There will be three groups, each with 20 to 25 brokers.
Winners:	In each group, the broker with the highest percentage increase of LAUNDEX case sales for the first quarter of 1994 versus the same period for 1993 will win.
Award:	The three winners will attend the United Airlines Tournament of Champions tennis match in Greenlefe, Florida—all expenses paid for two.
Mailings:	All magazines will be sent from a central location. Regional managers will supply buyers' names and addresses.

SCHEDULE:

Date	Action
Early January:	Brokers will get announcement of contest and running shoes to get them "off and running." Shortly after, they will get explanatory letters and LAUNDEX samples.
Late January:	Brokers will bring buyers a complimentary issue of one of the five promotion magazines featuring the LAUNDEX ad.
End of March:	All magazines will have been mailed.
April 10:	The awards will be announced.

Please note the schedule part of the memo above. This design will work for you whenever you have a chronological history of events, as in this example:

June 4:	You returned your recorder for repair.
June 8:	We called to give you an estimate.
June 12:	We received your letter asking us to proceed.

Remember to separate issues and action statements as in the rewrite below.

original:

There are a number of critical administrative issues that need to be addressed at this time.

1. Status meeting—As a follow-up to my voice mail, the Allied status meeting will be held on Monday, January 29, 3:00–5:00 p.m. in room 244. As always, along with the agenda, copies of the Pursuit profiles and the summary of the action items will be distributed. If you would like to discuss an individual action item or the responses to it, please bring copies.
2. ARMS—Updated, accurate reporting of ARMS is essential. Please contact your team leaders if you are unsure of the number of hours you should be spending on the Barclay project. I need this information at the latest by the time of our Monday meeting in order to review and correct any changes.

rewrite:

We need to address these issues.

ISSUE ONE—ALLIED STATUS MEETING

ACTIONS:

- As a follow-up to my voice mail, we will meet on Monday, January 29, 3:00–5:00 p.m. in room 244.
- We will distribute copies of the Pursuit profiles and the summary of the action items.
- If you want to discuss an item or responses to it, please bring copies.

ISSUE TWO—NEED FOR UPDATED, ACCURATE REPORTING OF ARMS

ACTIONS:

- Contact your team leaders if you aren't sure of how many hours to spend on the Barclay project.
- Give me your hour total by Monday, January 29—at the latest.

You'll notice that the rewrite adds a specific date on which you'll need the information. Since the last thing we read is the first thing we remember, it's always a good idea to end with this kind of specific note.

9

Write Proposals That Win for You Every Time

To communicate, put your thoughts in order; give them a purpose; use them to persuade, to instruct, to discover, to seduce.

—*William Safire*
Columnist, The New York Times

General Guidelines for Writing Proposals

1. Show your understanding of the client's problem.
2. Sell your product or service by stressing your concrete advantages over the competition—up front.
3. Explain:

   - Why your staff is effective
   - How the project will be managed
   - Who will be part of the team
   - What degree of responsibility each participant will have
   - How much impact the client will have on the project

4. Detail all time and money issues, noting any special terms and conditions or exceptions to their request for proposal (RFP).
5. Focus on results, and add some information on what will happen after the project is completed.

6. Make sure your proposal is neat and consistent in style.
7. Proofread for correctness and clarity. Have someone not familiar with your company's work and language read the whole proposal to ensure that it makes sense.

Kinds of Proposals

Internal

This is a persuasive document aimed at convincing management to accept an idea or project. Here's an example of a proposal for a new copier.

NEED FOR A NEW COPIER

OBJECTIVE

To purchase a copier that will produce large numbers of copies in a short time with a minimum amount of maintenance. It should contain stapling, collating, and double-sided features to save time and reduce paper cost.

RECOMMENDATION

The Konica 3135

BACKGROUND/JUSTIFICATION

Our current copier, the Konica 2203, has exceeded the manufacturer's recommended use. We can't fix the machine, since the manufacturer no longer produces the required parts (see enclosed letter).

During the past two years, we have called Konica on the average of every two weeks, causing disruption in work (see attached information on incidence and cost of repairs). Since we purchased the copier, our group has grown by 48%, with a corresponding growth in need for copies.

BENEFIT OF THE KONICA 3135

This copier will staple and collate. In addition, it can produce double-sided copies and copy large numbers of documents in a short time.

Its "code only accessibility" feature will regulate who can use the machine, which would in turn prevent personal copies being made during work hours and allow us to monitor how many copies are made.

COST ESTIMATES

See attached.

External—Solicited Proposal

Here you're responding to an RFP or an RFQ (request for quote).

Follow the solicitor's proposal requirements—including the problem, proposed solution, work needed, equipment to be supplied, time, and money issues.

Use the same outline and language the client has used in its printed guidelines.

External—Unsolicited Proposal

In this case, you're marketing to clients without any published guidelines to follow. Convince the reader you're aware of the particular nature of the problem and that you're prepared to solve it.

Design Elements for Any Proposal

- Title page
- Cover letter
- Executive summary
- Table of contents (for a longer proposal)
- Problem/need statement
- Solution/benefits
- Personnel
- Time and cost details
- Conclusion/recommendation (optional)

Title Page

Usually the RFP spells out what information should be included on this page. Typically you would include these elements:

- Title
- Client's name and address
- Person who signed the RFP
- Name of your company and address
- Person submitting
- Proposal number
- Date the proposal is due

Cover Letter

Avoid the typical "thank you for the opportunity" kind of opening. Instead, select a strong opening that personalizes you and makes you stand out as a winning competitor.

Offer your client a central selling point that creates strong appeal. Focus on benefits you have to offer and, if appropriate, briefly mention any special actions you took to identify their special needs.

In your closing, offer a contact person and number for your reader to call. Avoid using overworked phrases like "If you need any further information, do not hesitate to call."

good example of a cover letter

Dear Ms. Blake:

I enjoyed talking with you about your training needs this week, and I'm eager to get started designing a program that will work for you and your staff.

As we discussed, you've recently hired six new sales associates who have excellent sales skills but limited experience in writing letters. Specifically, they need the following:

Grammar update
Effective openings and closings
Improved page design techniques
Updated information on persuasive writing and tone

Our general approach to working on-site is listed below. Please note, though, that we can change the details in any way you like to meet your needs.

STEP ONE—NEEDS ANALYSIS
We'll ask you for background data (samples of letters, information on your client group, your goals, etc.) so we can determine your training needs and define your objectives.

We may ask to meet with key managers and staff or provide questionnaires and surveys.

STEP TWO—DEVELOPMENT
Using our extensive resources combined with the data you provide, we'll design a training program that's just right for you. We'll also select a course leader with at least ten years' experience in business writing—and an overall track record of excellence.

STEP THREE—DELIVERY
We'll deliver the materials and conduct the training at your site—on a date or dates convenient for you and your staff.

STEP FOUR—EVALUATION
Following the program, we'll collect evaluations from all participants and summarize them in a final report for you.

I'm enclosing some information on related programs and products for you to consider. Last year we delivered successful custom programs for more than 1,200 satisfied clients. We're pleased to share our expertise and vast resources with Allied as well.

I'd like to meet with you to discuss our proposed approach and also to go over our price structure. Would Friday, July 13 work for you? I'll call you this Tuesday morning to discuss a convenient date and time.

Meantime, please call me anytime with any questions. I'll be delighted to answer them.

Executive Summary

If you've ever read an abstract for a scientific article, you've seen all the key points of the article spelled out in advance. That's the function of the executive summary—to act as a mini-proposal for those who want the bottom line up front.

This summary details your objectives and your techniques for carrying them out. You highlight all procedures, plus cost/time/personnel considerations.

Most important, you stress the advantages and benefits you have to offer early in the proposal. Many companies decide whether or not to read a proposal on the basis of this summary, so you want to make sure you're complete and correct in this critical section.

Table of Contents

Used for longer proposals, this includes a list of tables and illustrations, as well as all elements included in the proposal.

Problem/Need Statement

Define the problem or issue to be addressed, being sure to note that you understand all its ramifications.

If you're eliminating environmental hazards, is there an OSHA inspection planned? If so, that would involve a deadline for your work. Also, what obstacles might arise that would add to the problem? How might you overcome them?

While you're defining the client's problem or need, identify the scope of the project. How extensive will you be in probing the issues? For an environmental project, how much of the site will you update? For a training program, how many employees will take part? And how flexible will you be in extending the number of participants?

Solution/Benefits

Explain what you're going to do and how you will do it, focusing on the benefits of your product or service. Be specific and realistic as to what you can accomplish and how you can meet your goals. Note what equipment you have and what you can get if needed.

Personnel

There are two parts to this section:

1. Include the various groups who will work on the project, detailing what role they play within your company. Note what percentage of their work time they will devote to your project.

2. In a separate biographical section, highlight the qualifications of each person who will play an active role in the project. Mention their success with other similar projects as you focus on their backgrounds, experience, and talents.

You'll want to place particular emphasis on the project director and project associates. They will direct the work and establish an important working relationship once the proposal is accepted.

While you're at it, include some information on how you will ensure that the client will be satisfied with both your implementation and follow-up. Also, include contingency plans if deadlines can't be met or personnel are not available.

Will the client's personnel be working with you? Note their potential role. If vendors will be involved, mention who will manage their schedule.

Finally, you may want to offer a brief history of your firm, noting any unique qualities that will benefit the client and the project. If requested, include references from satisfied previous customers (with their permission, of course).

Time and Budget Information

Organizations often specify how they want the budget presented. While some sections are presented in tabular form, you should include a "budget justification" segment that states your rationale for your financial figures, in paragraph form.

As you discuss costs, stay within their budget framework, including all actual costs plus projected expenses. Anything you can throw in as value-added will work to your advantage. If you're asked to submit a bid, avoid going in too low, as you may be perceived as having very little to offer.

Here is a sample of a budget table.

SIX-MONTH BUDGET

PERSONNEL

Budget director, 25% of time	$_____
Project associate, 15%	_____
Assistant, 50%	_____

Clerk-typist, part-time	————
Staff benefits (20% of salary and wages)	————
CONSULTANTS	————
MATERIALS	————
Office supplies	————
Construction materials	————
TRAVEL	
Two people to client site, air and expenses	————
TOTAL DIRECT COSTS	————
INDIRECT COSTS (60% of	
total direct costs)	————
GRAND TOTAL	————

Writing and Presentation Issues

1. Translate technical information into language a nontechnical reader can appreciate and understand.
2. Avoid jargon unless you're sure all readers understand your usage.
3. Keep your title simple and make sure it clearly identifies your project subject.
4. Consider hiring an artist to prepare your cover and illustrations.
5. Review for completeness. Be specific in backing up any claims with concrete information on how you will follow through.
6. Edit carefully to eliminate unnecessary language. As long as you're complete, you want to state your points in the simplest language possible.

Here are some examples of how you can simplify your language and make it more appealing.

original:

The work effort in Phase One may be reusable during Phases Two and Three, thereby reducing the effort necessary to complete these phases.

rewrite:

We may be able to shorten the second and third phases by reusing some of the efforts from the first phase.

original:

For each phase of the implementation, Allied will use its proven implementation methodology and a defined work plan to assist Acme in the implementation.

rewrite:

Allied will draw on both its experience and its work plan to help Acme during each phase of the implementation. [*You might consider saying "We will draw on both our experience and our work plan to help you during each phase of the implementation."*]

original:

The consulting work will be performed on a time and material basis, allowing both Allied and Acme the flexibility in the day-to-day direction of the work. If additional consulting days are required, Allied shall be compensated for the related services.

rewrite:

All consulting will be done on a time and material basis—allowing more flexible direction of daily activities. Allied will be compensated for any added consulting days not already noted in the budget.

original:

This estimated cost does not include reasonable travel and living expenses, which Acme is expected to pay. For budgeting purposes, we have found from experience that travel and living expenses can be expected to be about 12% of the incurred professional fees. Allied will make its best efforts to staff the engagement with local resources although it may be necessary to use nonlocal resources from time to time.

rewrite:

Acme will be responsible for reasonable travel and living expenses not mentioned in the estimate, which our experience shows will be about 12% of the professional fees. We will try to use local personnel whenever possible to limit these costs.

PART TWO

Sample Account Management Letters and Internal Documents

Follow-Up to a Meeting/Action Plan

I came back all fired up from our meeting yesterday. After seeing your space and the exciting design possibilities, I certainly share your eagerness to get the project started.

As we discussed, we'll send you a preliminary plan on March 18, covering furniture, lighting, and equipment. I know you'll be pleased with our prices. No one buys in greater bulk than we do, and we're pleased to pass our cost savings on to you.

After you have reviewed the plan, I'll get our staff together so that we can iron out the final details. You have already met Sheila and Bob. They have asked me to let you know how thrilled they are to be working with you.

Thanks, Dan, for allowing Office Mart to submit a proposal. If there's anything I've left out or if you have any questions, please give me a call anytime.

Response to an Inquiry

I'm pleased to send you our pamphlet on "Purchasing Property in Westchester," which you requested in September.

As parents of children of school age, you'll be particularly interested in pages 10–12, which discuss school systems in the area. Naturally, property values are tied in to school reputation.

After you read the pamphlet, you may have some questions about which area will best suit your needs. I'm ready and eager to answer them—and to show you around our beautiful countrified towns.

Call me anytime, Barbara. I have at least five homes that I think will be perfect for you.

A Gracious Offer of Repair

We appreciate your kind note of June 4 expressing your delight with the camera you received at one of our workshops.

You mentioned that your latest pictures haven't been as clear as the previous ones. There could be many reasons for this problem.

Just mail the camera, enclosing your name and address, to our letterhead address, and mark it to my attention. We'll be pleased to handle the repair at no cost to you.

Real Estate Letter

Next year, about 12,000 people in your area will sell their homes. Some will make a profit, while others will suffer a loss.

If you're considering a move, here are three reasons you should turn to Best Acres Realty as your agent.

First, we've sold more homes and commercial real estate than anyone else in the state—10 percent more than our nearest competitor. So we have the clout and background to make the sale.

Second, we know how to ensure that you make a profit—from fixing up your home and property to implementing techniques for satisfying even the fussiest prospective buyer.

Third—and most important—we're small and very service-oriented. Have a question? You'll be sure to get a complete and knowledgeable answer from us right away, day or night. We'll make the whole process a simple and comfortable reality for you.

Let's talk—now or anytime you're in the market to sell.

Letter to a New Customer—Request for Action

WELCOME TO STRICKLANDS. . . .

We certainly appreciate your order for 30 warm-up suits, Mr. Lippmann, and are pleased to welcome you as a customer. We'll do everything we can to live up to your expectations of our quality and our service.

To make sure your order arrives quickly, I'm shipping this first order to you by Express mail this afternoon. Please fill out the enclosed credit form so we can handle your future orders without delay.

Your credit information will, of course, be kept confidential. May we have this by June 13?

We look forward to working with you.

Letter When You Have Lost a Customer

We haven't seen you lately . . . and we've missed you.

Your account has been quiet for the past year—no purchases, no activity at all.

If we've done something to upset you, please let us know. If our merchandise no longer pleases you, we'd like to hear about this, too.

Your business and your friendship are important to us. If you've just been busy lately, we'd like you to make a little time to come in and see our new line of designer suits. Please use the enclosed discount coupon for any purchase. It's our way of saying we're happy to see you back at Carter's.

Letter to a New Customer

We are pleased to open a credit account for you, as you requested in your letter of July 9.

Just for your information, we're including some literature about our credit policies and finance charges for late payments.

Now for the good news. As a regular charge customer, you'll be able to shop during our sales before the general public can. You'll receive special discount coupons and have the chance to earn special gifts (and gift certificates) based on the amount you spend each year.

As a way of saying "welcome," we're enclosing a 15 percent savings coupon for you to use now through September 15 in any department in the store.

Enjoy your first purchase and all those that follow.

Unusual Pitch for Business

Have you ever agonized over what to get your wife for her birthday? Even worse, have you ever forgotten her birthday? (Now there's a sin that's hard to live down.)

If either of these possibilities strikes a familiar chord, we'd like to do two things to help.

First, we'd like to remind you that your wife's birthday is Tuesday, August 20. Second, since she's a regular customer and our sales associates are aware of her likes and dislikes, we'd be happy to have one of them pick out a gift for her from you.

If this suggestion appeals, please call Virginia Frank any weekday at 246-3200. She'll be delighted to make some suggestions in any price range YOU choose.

Thank-You Note for Hospitality

Thank you for your gracious hospitality during my visit to Los Angeles last week. I enjoyed everything about my stay, but dinner at your home was a particular treat. Jean will be gratified to hear that her recipe for lamb was a big hit with my family. Please extend my thanks to her, too.

I really appreciate your kindness, Jack.

Announcement of New Staff-1

I'm pleased to note a very special addition to our sales team, Rick Algato. Rick will take over for Margaret Kropp, who has recently transferred to our Chicago branch.

Rick comes to us from Johnson & Sandborn, where he sold digital routers for seven years. He's very familiar with our product and is eager to get started with us.

I know Rick will appreciate your warm welcome and any help you can give him as he gets to know us.

We all wish Rick much success. We're fortunate to have him on the team.

Announcement of New Staff-2

Effective March 16, Emanuel Zorich will join our department as a systems analyst reporting to Lois Spence.

Manny, as he prefers to be called, worked previously at Higgins Blaine, also as a systems analyst. He's a graduate of New York University, with advanced degrees in computer technology. When not hard at work, Manny can be found running in a marathon or two and playing duplicate bridge (we're all most impressed that he has achieved the rank of Life Master). His wife, Rita, is a high school math teacher.

Please join me in welcoming Manny to our staff. He wants you to know he'd love to have you drop by his office on the fourth floor any time—just to say hi or even to help him unpack a few boxes.

Follow-Up Letter When the Customer Hasn't Responded

In the rush of work, you probably haven't had time to review my recent letter, which pinpointed how our Easy Dial System can help you improve your communication with your customers. Just in case my letter didn't reach you, I'm enclosing a copy.

Our offer to waive the ordinary start-up fee of $75 expires January 25. I will call you Tuesday morning to discuss how we can save you time and money through Easy Dial. Or give me a call before then whenever you have a moment. I'd love to hear from you.

Letter About an Upcoming Meeting

weak:

We are very pleased that you will be joining us on May 18 to discuss the possible uses of photography in your business.

Our group will consist of 15 to 20 people from all over the country, giving us and you the opportunity to get a national perspective on the insurance agency business.

The meeting, cocktail reception, and dinner will be held at the Sheraton Waikiki Hotel. The hotel does not assign hotel suites ahead of time, so please check the electronic board of the hotel for the meeting's suite number. Please fill out the enclosed questionnaire and return it to us as soon as possible in the envelope provided.

You will be receiving a check for $100 in consideration for your time. It is important to include your Social Security number on the enclosed form so that we can properly process your check.

rewrite:

> We're pleased that you'll be joining us on May 18 to discuss the possible uses of photography in your business.
>
> Our group will consist of 15 to 20 people from all over the country, giving us and you the chance to get a national perspective on the insurance agency business.
>
> The meeting, cocktail reception, and dinner will be held at the Sheraton Waikiki Hotel.
>
> ACTION ITEMS
> 1. Check the hotel's electronic board for the meeting's suite number (the hotel doesn't assign rooms ahead of time).
> 2. Fill out the enclosed questionnaire and return it in the envelope provided <u>by April 4.</u>
> 3. Include your Social Security number on this form. You'll be receiving a check for $100 to thank you for your time, and we want to be sure it's processed correctly.
>
> See you on the 18th!

Letter of Explanation to Sales Force

original:

Three (3) separate sample shipments will be arriving at your home over the next three (3) weeks. We apologize for the inconvenience in coordinating receipt and signature for the samples, but it cannot be helped. We recognize that this business of three (3) separate shipments increases costs and cuts down on sales time, but please just bear with it.

A shipment of excess Topcal samples may already be in your possession. On or about April 20, a one-time shipment of Forte samples will be arriving. This will be the only Forte shipment until November, so plan accordingly. This shipment is cycle four & five's allotment. Your normal third-cycle shipment of the product line, including Alvex, will be arriving by May 1. As per the sales plan, the amount of Alvex samples will vary dependent upon the size of each territory sales volume and quota.

As per our policy, please count the samples and enter the inventory in your laptop computer. Some of the Forte samples are actually mail samples. Each sleeve contains four (4) sample trays. Please consider each tray as a separate sample. For example, one mail sample = four (4) samples in the laptop.

rewrite:

Here is some information about the three separate sample shipments that will arrive at your home over the next three weeks. We appreciate your bearing with the difficulty in coordinating receipts and signatures for the separate shipments. The schedule is as follows:

- You may already have received the Topcal samples.
- About April 20, allotment of Forte samples for cycles four and five will arrive as a one-time shipment (the only one in November, so plan accordingly).
- By May 1, your normal third-cycle product line—including Alvex—will arrive. According to the sales plan, the amount of Alvex samples will vary by territory sales and quotas.

Please follow our policy by counting the samples and entering them into your laptop.

Note: Some Forte samples are actually mail samples in which each sleeve has four trays. Consider each tray as a separate sample. For example:

one mail sample = four samples in the laptop.

Technical Recommendation

original:

Dear Mark and Jerry:

If BYD performs the concept testing screening for both your categories simultaneously, there can be a substantial financial savings. Please let me explain.

Earlier in November, I sent you separate proposals to conduct concept testing with similar screening requirements. For Jerry's research, we would screen the panel with ½-page InstaVue to 20,000 households to find a sample of Mystic and non-Mystic buyers. For Mark's we would also use a ½-page of InstaVue, but due to a lower incidence (compared to Jerry's research), we would need to mail to 25,000 households because your needs are a little more complex—Mark's sample of Mystic buyers' and non-buyers' needs to be stratified by store type.

We should combine both screeners into ½-page InstaVue and mail to 35,000 households. This would provide enough samples for both concept tests and save you over $4,000—$15,700 versus $20,000 for both screeners.

rewrite:

Dear Mark and Jerry:

I'd like to explain why you'll save money if we perform the concept testing screening for both your categories simultaneously.

For Jerry:	We'd screen the panel with one $\frac{1}{2}$-page InstaVue to 20,000 households for a sample of Mystic and non-Mystic buyers.
For Mark:	We'd use the same $\frac{1}{2}$-page, but we'd need to mail to 25,000 households because your needs are more complex (you need to stratify by store type).

RECOMMENDATION:

We should combine both screeners into one $\frac{1}{2}$-page of InstaVue and mail it to 35,000 households. This would give you enough samples for both tests and save you over $4,000 ($15,700 versus $20,000).

Announcement to Clients

We're pleased to tell you that Proxy International (PI) will provide all international proxy voting services for you from now on. We have engaged this firm because of its superb service record.

WHAT IS PI?

This international investment services firm manages global proxy voting operations for financial institutions and large investors. Founded in 1980, PI is active in 60 countries—with a portfolio that includes $50 billion of international equities.

WHAT CAN PI OFFER YOU?

- More detailed agenda information with no increase in proxy fees
- Ability to accept standing instructions
- Daily reporting to clients
- Expanded voting capabilities (from 38 to 48 countries)

Enclosed are copies of reports similar to those PI will begin sending you soon, plus a copy of PI's standard instruction handbook. Please look them over—and give us a call anytime to discuss this valuable new service.

A Thank-You to a Coworker

Greg, you and your group have done an outstanding job in clearing up the problems we were having with our packaging at the Peabody plant. Don't think your efforts have gone unnoticed in speeding up the box production. We were all amazed at how much you have accomplished in so short a time.

Our customers thank you, our factory workers thank you, and I thank you. Great job!

We Didn't Get the Account

It's true that we didn't get the Olympic account. It's equally true that ours was the best presentation—and we should have no regrets.

Who knows what prompted their decision to go with Merrill instead of us? I certainly don't know—it could easily have been some factor beyond our control.

What I'm concerned about now is that you be proud of what you put together and as happy with the team as I am.

Keep up the super work—and next time it will be our turn!

Information Letter to a Concerned Stockholder

Thank you for letting us know about the loss of your stock certificate #TV-10900 for 400 shares of common stock. We've already issued a stock transfer notation, and it's a simple process from here to issue a new certificate for you.

Please do the following to speed up your replacement.

1. Sign all three copies of the enclosed Affidavit of Loss.
2. Send us a check for $280 payable to the Norback Surety Company. They will assume liability for the lost certificate under our Blanket Loss Securities Bond.

As soon as these steps are completed, we'll immediately send your new certificate to you.

We Didn't Get the Business Because We Didn't Do the Job

About the Hopkins deal.

I don't agree with Bill Neeck, who, as president of the Chicago White Sox, was quoted as saying, "I do not think that winning is the most important thing. I think winning is the only thing."

Well, to my mind, preparation and follow-up are the only things. If we've done our job, we can be at ease with the results—win or lose. Unfortunately, we weren't prepared, and we certainly didn't follow up with Hopkins.

Here's what we didn't do:

- <u>Spend enough time at Hopkins to find out what their business needs were.</u> Our suggestion for them to change their catalog was vague and embarrassing.
- <u>Proofread our proposal.</u> Carmen Fernandez told me this morning that our work was sloppy, filled with typos.
- <u>Do the research.</u> We sounded foolish suggesting a "new" concept of telemarketing that's been around for over a year.

We learned a costly lesson with this account. Now let's put it behind us and move on—and I mean move on so we're ready to be winners the next time around.

Congratulations—We Got the Job

"The breakfast of champions is not cereal, it's the opposition, it's the opposition."

> —Nick Seitz, Editor of *Golf Digest*

Well, we chewed our opposition up, and boy . . . doesn't winning feel great!

We've always known our products were superior. But it's good to have the client confirm this fact by choosing us over all the rest.

When your feet reach the ground again (tomorrow), you'll need to get to work. Here's the schedule:

Date	Activity
Tuesday, November 4:	We're meeting with Jim Donahue and Eliza Gold to set up a production schedule.
Friday, November 7:	The specs are due for the fabric.
Wednesday, November 12:	The client will sign off on the fabric.
Monday, November 17:	The assignments will be ready. Clear your decks before then.

Be proud of the job you've done. My best congratulations to all.

Memo to the Team About Disappointing Revenues

Paul "Bear" Bryant, as a football coach, had this to say:

"If anything goes bad, I did it.
"If anything goes semi-good, then we did it.
"If anything goes real good, then you did it."

I'd rather take the blame than point fingers about what happened last quarter. Instead of bemoaning our fate, I'd like to focus on how we can turn things around.

Here are three suggestions to help you sell at or above quota. Write them on your hand if you must. They will turn the tide.

1. <u>Focus on benefits as you sell.</u> Remember, the customer has a wide range of products to choose from. We have the best product, so be specific in highlighting what's in it for them.
2. <u>Follow up client visits with a phone call and note.</u> Don't wait for clients to call you. I'm enclosing four model phone conversations and letters—adapt them to fit your needs.
3. <u>Make sure your customer service is as good as we promise.</u> We respond to complaints immediately. If we don't have an answer, we say so and give an estimate of when we will.

Our mission is clear. Our product is the best. I know that soon things will be going "real good" and <u>you</u> will have done it.

Sympathy for a Bad Result

Well, you didn't get the Duane account, and I have to say we were all surprised and disappointed for you. You put so much time and energy into your presentation.

Let's look at the bright side. You made some good friends at Duane. Who knows what will happen next year? I'm counting on you, Bob, to come out a winner next time.

Note When They Chose a Competitor

You picked an excellent group for your ad campaign by selecting AFG. And while I wish it had been us, I understand what you liked in their presentation.

Thanks for considering us, Jackie. We wish you great success with your campaign.

Letter to Handle a Problem

Just when you thought you had set up your payroll system to run flawlessly, you add several new employees and decide to change some of your benefits.

The Quick-Adjust system we have developed allows you to switch payroll tracks in a matter of minutes.

Do you have five minutes free next Tuesday morning to discuss how inexpensive and easy-to-use our system is? I'll call you at 10:00 a.m. to give you a quick summary of our benefits.

Letter When a Customer Has Had a Business Disaster

> We were very sorry to hear about the fire in your factory on Tuesday.
>
> There may be something we can do to help. We have some extra storage space in the basement of our Main Street store. Please let me know if you'd like to use this or if there's anything else you need.
>
> You've been a good friend and customer for a long time. And we want you to know we're here for you now.

Sympathy for a Death in the Family

> It was with great sadness that I learned this morning about your recent loss. I valued Mark's friendship over the past twenty years. His sense of humor, commitment to excellence, and obvious integrity were recognized and very much appreciated by everyone who worked with him. We will all sorely miss him.
>
> My deepest sympathy to you and your family. If there is anything I can do to help in the coming weeks, please be sure to let me know.

Request

weak:

> We, at Allied, are very interested in making a technical presentation to the Sun-Up Production Advisory Committee (PAC), regarding our state-of-the-art Allied bottle-handling system. We increasingly believe that this advanced bottling system will add significant value through improved bottle-line efficiency and increased production uptime.
>
> When we met recently in Atlanta, Georgia, we discussed the PAC meeting that will occur in Dallas on October 4 and 5. What is the potential for Allied to make a technical presentation of our new program to the key Sun-Up Production Leadership Team? If the schedule opportunity exists for the October meeting, would you please add Allied to that agenda.
>
> Rich, please provide your direction on this matter as soon as possible. As always, your assistance is greatly appreciated.

rewrite:

> I need your help concerning the PAC meeting coming up in Dallas on October 4–5. When we met in Atlanta, we discussed this meeting—and here's my question.
>
> Is there a chance we can make a technical presentation to Sun-Up on our new, advanced bottling system? We'd like the chance to show the key Sun-Up Production Leadership Team how our system will improve bottle-line efficiency and increase production uptime.
>
> Rich, please do your best to add Allied to the meeting agenda. As always, I greatly appreciate everything you do for us.

Upbeat Advertising Letter

It's hard to believe that a new year is upon us. Only a few short months ago, KFFW in Houston changed affiliations from CBS to FOX, becoming the fourth-rated FOX affiliate in the country. What a difference a quarter makes!

You had the foresight to utilize the powerful KFFW-KDSI combo as the cornerstone of your Houston buys, and I'm pleased to tell you that your intuition paid off in a major way. KFFW continues to show an upward growth trend in key dayparts.

Lisa, as we begin 1997, I want to thank you for your continued support. We are proud to be the stations you turn to when you place your advertising dollars in Houston, and we pride ourselves on being stations that deliver.

We look forward to a mutually prosperous 1997!

Letter Soliciting Business

There's a lot to be said about going with what you know. So I would understand if you were thinking of staying with your current vendor.

But let me give you another perspective. Familiarity sometimes leads to dull thinking and stagnant motivation.

I'd like the chance to show you some of our creative thoughts on your project. Change can be a good thing—and we're certainly motivated.

Can we get together to talk about this?

Customer Service Letter

weak:

I have been unable to reach you by telephone regarding your request to investigate some overdrafts. Our research shows that there were two $200 overdrafts from your checking account on May 4 and June 4. The problem was corrected on June 6.

We have enclosed a $400 check, which represents the total amount of the overdrafts. We also will reimburse you for any overdraft charges incurred due to these erroneous transactions.

I sincerely regret any inconvenience or concern this situation may have caused you. Please contact me if you have any questions regarding the matter.

We appreciate your investment and want to assure you we will make every effort to provide optimal service in the future.

rewrite:

I'd like to update you about the overdrafts you alerted us to. You're right. We did mistakenly charge you $200 in May and June. Here's what we've done about this problem.

First, we corrected the account on June 6. Also, we've enclosed a check for $400 for the overdrafts and will pay you back for any related charges.

Most important, we sincerely apologize for our carelessness in handling your account. There's no excuse for you to receive anything less than perfect service from us. I did try to call you to express this thought more personally but couldn't reach you.

We do appreciate your business and will work hard to make sure all your future dealings with us are perfect.

Cover Letter to a Proposal

weak:

Attached for your review and solicitation of comments is a proposal to introduce the concept of photo imaging technology and how it would be utilized in your management of paper documents.

The benefits:

- Paper documents would be available for warehousing, off premises, within days reducing the space needed for on-site storage and <u>it's</u> related costs.   **no apostrophe when *its* is possessive**
- Turnaround time for producing hard copy documents would be reduced dramatically as a result of quickened access time.
- Staff requirements would be less since there would be no re-files of previously retrieved records.
- Warehouse location of paper documents would be readily determined from the electronic index in the event physical retrieval is required.

rewrite:

We're pleased to introduce photo imaging technology and to explain how you can use this exciting process to manage your paper documents.

Benefits:
- Reduce on-site storage space needs by having paper documents available for warehousing off-site within days.
- Reduce turnaround time for producing hard copy documents from inquiry requests, based on faster access time.
- Save time and staff by avoiding refiling of previously retrieved records.
- Find warehouse location of paper documents easily from the electronic index if physical retrieval is needed.

Cover Letter to a Proposal

wordy:

Attached is an outline of the new Quick Touch Phone System. We would like to offer this service as part of an overall package for your client, Frugal Rental Cars. It is truly an innovative and extremely valuable service. The premise is simple. If a person needs a Frugal car, chances are he or she is a business traveler using it in another city.

Quick Touch is a toll-free information hot line. It is a perfect venue to capture prospective business travelers. Reaching a total of 500,000 people, Quick Touch is an instantaneous database that viewers access with their phones. Sports scores, entertainment updates, and weather forecasts are but some of the reasons why thousands have already used our service.

What we propose is Frugal's sponsorship of one of our most popular segments, the weather forecast for travelers. Callers will be encouraged to access more detailed information about Frugal products. Should the caller need to rent a car immediately, our system will transfer the call directly to Frugal's line. The real strength of Quick Touch is its ability to track leads.

I would like to discuss this system further with you. I will call you next week to get your impressions of the system.

rewrite:

We'd like to offer our new Quick Touch Phone System as part of an overall package for Frugal Rental Cars. As you can see in the attached outline, the premise of this innovative service is simple.

Anyone who needs a Frugal rental car is likely to be a business traveler away from home. And that's where Quick Touch comes in.

What is Quick Touch?

It's a toll-free information hot line that reaches 500,000 people. It's also an instant database viewers access with their phones—for sports scores, entertainment updates, and weather forecasts.

Here's what we propose:

- Frugal will sponsor one of our most popular segments, the weather forecast for travelers.
- Callers will be encouraged to access detailed information about Frugal products.
- If someone wants to rent a car, the system will transfer the call directly to Frugal's line.
- Most important, the system is able to track leads.

I'll give you a call Monday to discuss how you can put this valuable system to work for your clients.

Request-for-Action Letter

weak:

We, at Allied, greatly appreciate the opportunity to supply closures and technical equipment to the Acme Company of the Southwest. Our goal as a company is to be an integral part of your application system.

Enclosed please find a revised copy of our original closure supply agreement for your review and signature. Per my discussion with Amanda Strang February 1, 1996, minor modifications have been made. The new agreement is in effect as of March 20, 1996, for a period of three years. All modifications are marked with an arrow sticker and subject to your approval. Please advise immediately if there are any questions or issues regarding the agreement.

Please sign the enclosed copies and return them to my attention, at which time Grace and I will sign them and return the original to you. Your assistance in this matter is greatly appreciated.

rewrite:

> We're pleased you have chosen us to supply you with closures and technical equipment.
>
> There are just a few details left to work out for the enclosed closure supply agreement. As I discussed with Amanda Strang on February 1, we have made some minor changes (marked with an arrow sticker). The new version will be in effect as of March 20, 1996, for three years.
>
> Please let me know if you have any questions or concerns. Otherwise, sign both copies and return them to me by February 24. Grace and I will sign them and return the original to you.
>
> Thank you for taking care of this, Les. We're eager to get started on making a valuable contribution to your application system.

Response to a Letter of Inquiry

> I'm pleased to answer your questions about part-time employees and the retirement system.
>
> First, you asked who decides whether someone is part-time concerning eligibility for the system. We usually accept the employer's determination.
>
> Then you asked about your coaches. You'd be safer to call them part-time employees and give them the choice of joining the system. Please note: If they don't want to joint, you'll need to submit an IRA waiver to the system each year so you won't be liable for contributions.
>
> Please write again if you need any other information.

Summary Letter

weak:

This letter recaps the issues discussed and responds to the action items assigned to AMR during our status meeting on Wednesday, August 7.

AMR has reviewed the list of action items and has determined that the information now requested by BBT is similar to AMR's original proposal, which was modified to its current state. In summary, BBT is requesting a price quotation for the following:

- AMR will revisit each of the facilities located throughout the U.S. to conduct a complete cable plant analysis. The objective is to determine whether the existing cable infrastructure is usable.
- For each site visited, AMR will provide BBT with cable routes, split pair listing, and termination types.

The cost for all work is $135 per hour plus all travel costs

Feel **is weaker than** *believe.*

and expenses. We <u>feel</u> that providing an hourly rate is more cost-effective, since each of the sites varies in size and complexity. Estimated time to complete the task is five (<u>5</u>) weeks.

Don't repeat numbers.

Jack, it is our opinion that the on-site analysis proposed will provide your group with the information they need to complete the M-Power roll-out. We look forward to meeting with you again to discuss this further. Please call me with any questions.

improved:

I'd like to recap the action items we discussed in our status meeting on August 7.

The information BBT is requesting is similar to what AMR's original proposal outlined (now modified).

Here are the details.

AMR'S ACTIONS
- Revisit each U.S. facility, analyzing the whole cable plant to see if the existing cable infrastructure is usable.
- Provide cable routes, split pair listing, and termination types for each site.

COST
The rate is $135 per hour, plus travel costs and expenses. We believe an hourly rate is more cost-effective, as each site varies in size and complexity.

ESTIMATED TIME TO COMPLETE THE WORK
Five weeks

Jack, we believe the proposed on-site analysis is just what your group needs to complete the M-Power roll-out.

We look forward to meeting again to iron out the details. Meantime, give me a call anytime with questions.

Saying No in a Sensitive Way

I'd like to respond to your recent request for claims experience data by explaining how we determine our group rates.

First, we must pool claims data for all customers with under 100 employees, like you. This complies with Illinois law and allows coverage for large claims without affecting rates.

Second, if we considered individual claims data, groups with good experience would leave us—and your rates would go up sharply.

For these reasons, it would not be in your best interest for us to supply the information you requested.

Please call if you'd like to discuss other ways to reduce your premiums. We have some good ideas for you, and we always enjoy hearing from you.

Mass Mailer to Investors

When you're self-employed, you're often too busy with day-to-day details of running your own business to think about saving for retirement. But as a self-employed person, you're responsible for planning your own retirement because there may be no corporate pension plan to fall back on.

December 29, 1998 is the deadline!

That's why it's important to consider how the Blackstrong Plan can help you save on taxes while you start to save for retirement.

Gain a Substantial Tax Deduction **This** Year
With our Plan, you can make a yearly tax-deductible contribution of as much as 25% of your earned income. What a great way to lower your taxable income year after year while you save for retirement.

Gain the Power of Tax-Deferred Growth **Every** Year
Any investment earnings grow tax-deferred until you begin making withdrawals. This can make a tremendous difference in the money you'll have at retirement.

We know that when you're in business for yourself, every moment counts. Please review all the options in our enclosed brochure. Any of our plans can make all your retirement fantasies a reality.

Call our 800 number anytime, 24 hours a day, to discuss investments with a representative or to request a prospectus. You'll be glad you did.

P.S. Remember: December 29 is your deadline for making your contribution this year. Don't delay!

Appendix

FIFTEEN GRAMMAR MISTAKES YOU DON'T WANT TO MAKE

1. *Given the background you provided on the new client; I think this feature is ideal.*
   You can't use a semicolon to join a phrase and an independent clause. Substitute a comma.
2. *You're right Nancy, about the concerns you have expressed.*
   Add a comma before *Nancy*. In direct address, use commas before and after a person's name.
3. *The program had it's best rating of the year.*
   Use an apostrophe with *its* only when you have a contraction of *it* plus *is* as in *It's raining*. Never use the apostrophe when *its* is possessive.
   By the way, there is no such word as *its'*.
4. *It's customers like yourself that help improve our business.*
   The correct word is *you*. You can appreciate yourself; I can only appreciate you.
5. *Gail asked Dwight and I to rewrite the report.*
   Change *I* to *me*. If you pretended Dwight's name wasn't there, you would always say *Gail asked* me *to rewrite the report*.
6. *The figures are cause for rejoicing. Once again proving we have the right techniques.*
   Replace the period with a comma, since you don't have two complete thoughts (the second concept is a phrase).
7. *Before coming to Tyler, Nie Lih worked at Metropolitan for a three year stint.*
   Add a hyphen between *three* and *year*. Compound adjectives

take hyphens when they come before a noun they jointly modify.

Examples: *Short-term gain*
Well-deserved criticism
Thank-you note

8. *George Baker, our best salesperson just left the firm.*
Add a comma after *salesperson*. You need commas around both sides of a phrase.

9. *The program is excellent, however, we're not sure it will work for us.*
Put a semicolon or period before *however*, and keep the comma after it.

10. *I would appreciate you doing the work for me.*
Change *you* to *your*.

11. *Our employees' are doing an excellent job.*
Don't use an apostrophe unless *employees* is possessive, which it isn't in the sentence above.

12. *The background and experience of all candidates has been assessed.*
Change *has* to *have*, since you have a compound subject.

13. *I was really anxious to hear from you about the sales report.*
Use *eager*. *Anxious* means worried.

14. *The format was alright, though we decided not to use it.*
Make *alright* two words—*all right. A lot* is also two words.

15. *A great amount of people attended the service.*
Use *number* for any items you can count and *amount* for bulk (amount of money).

PROOFREADING TECHNIQUES

1. Put your work aside for at least an hour before proofreading. The longer you wait, the more you'll notice typos or language that doesn't make sense.
2. Read aloud. That way you will hear if you sound stuffy or foolish.
3. Read backwards for language mistakes. If you read starting with the last word and moving backwards to the first word, you'll spend more time on each word—and pick up more errors.
4. Ask for help. If your skills are weak, it's important to have someone check for errors. Also, you might want a nontechnical person to read your work to see if your ideas make sense.

Practice Simplifying Your Language

Original	Translation
on a monthly basis	monthly
in the state of Maine	in Maine
for training purposes	for training
there are various issues	there are issues
we have specific concerns	we have concerns
we have definite ideas	we have ideas
many different areas	many areas
at a time when	when
the reason why	the reason
continue in the future	continue
in the event that	if
in need of	need
it is our opinion	we believe
in the amount of	for
in the process of	[eliminate this phrase]
due to the fact that	because
in an efficient way	efficiently
we reviewed four (4)	we reviewed four
long period of time	long time
in lieu of	instead of
achieve improvements	improve
red in color	red
approximately 20 to 30	about 25

Transitions You Can Use for a Smoother Flow

In the same direction: *and, also, besides, moreover, in addition, too, furthermore, another*

To show contrast: *however, but, on the other hand, even so, still, nevertheless, conversely*

To show result: *thus, therefore, so, consequently, as a result, for this reason, because of this*

Time orientation: *next, then, from now on, meanwhile, first, second, finally, after this, at the same time*

Illustration: *as an example, for instance, for example, in other words, what's more*

TROUBLESOME WORDS

advise/inform:	*Advise* is a pretentious way of saying *inform* or *tell*.
affect/effect:	*Affect* (verb) means "to influence," while *effect* (verb) means "to cause" or "to make happen."
aforementioned:	This sounds pompous. Say *this* or *that* instead.
agree:	You agree *with* a person; *to* a proposal; *on* a plan.
all right:	This is always two words; the same is true for *a lot.*
along the lines of:	Say *like* instead.
angry:	You're angry *at* something; *about* a situation; *with* a person.
anxious/eager:	*Anxious* suggests worried; if you're enthusiastic, use *eager.*
anybody:	This is always one word.
at a later date:	Save time by saying *later.*
at the present time:	Say *now* instead.
attached hereto:	This is old-fashioned and stuffy. Say *attached is* or *here is.*
because:	Don't use this with the word *reason.* "The reason we fired her was *that* (not *because*) she refused to work hard."
beside, besides:	*Beside* means "next to"; *besides* means "in addition to."
between you and me:	*Between you and I* is incorrect.
cannot:	This is one word.
can't hardly:	The correct usage is *can hardly.*

close proximity: This is redundant. Say one or the other.

continue on: Omit the word *on*.

different from: This is used with nouns and pronouns. "My sales plan is different from yours."

different than: Use this before a clause. "My sales plan is different than I had originally planned it to be."

disregardless: This word doesn't exist. Say *regardless*.

due to the fact that: This is wordy. Say *because* instead.

each: When *each* comes before a single noun or is the subject of the sentence, use a singular verb. "Each manager is expected to stay late" or "Each of us is expected to stay late."

e.g.:   This is a shorter way of saying *for example*.

enclose/inclose: These are used interchangeably, though *enclose* is more common.

end result: This is redundant. Say *result*.

estimated at about: Leave out *about*.

farther/further: Use *farther* when writing about measurable distance; use *further* when discussing an extension in time.

fewer in number: Leave out *in number*.

fewer/less: When referring to individual, countable items, use *fewer*; when referring to quantity, use *less*. "Fewer people, less work."

forgo/forego: *Forgo*, without an *e*, means "to give up" or "do without"; *forego*, with an *e*, means "to go before" or "precede."

for the purpose of:	Say *to*.
for the reason that:	Say *because*.
i.e.:	This introduces a definition and means "that is."
if and when:	Use one or the other.
imply/infer:	*Imply* means "to suggest" (give out information) and *infer* "to gather information" or "deduce." The writer *implies* while the reader *infers*.
in accordance with your request:	Say *as you requested*.
in connection with:	Say *about* or *concerning* instead.
in excess of:	Say *more than*.
in the amount of:	Say *for* instead.
in regard to:	Say *about* or *concerning*. *In regards to* is incorrect and should be avoided.
irregardless:	This word doesn't exist; say *regardless*.
its, it's:	*Its* suggests possession ("the dog wagged its tail"); *it's* is a contraction of *it* and *is* ("it's raining").
join together:	Eliminate *together*; it's redundant.
kindly:	Don't use this as a substitute for *please*.
last but not least:	Avoid using this old-fashioned phrase.
lie/lay:	*Lie* means to recline, *lay* to place.
neither:	This always takes a singular verb. "Neither of the men was able to do the work."
neither . . . nor:	Always use *nor* (not *or*) with *neither*.
new innovation:	Eliminate *new* (it's redundant).

no one:	These are always two words.
off of:	Eliminate *of*. "He took 15% off [not *off of*] the price."
past experience:	Eliminate *past;* all experience is from the past.
per (as in per your . . .):	Avoid using this pretentious word.
percent/percentage:	The term *percent* is specific and requires a definite figure; *percentage* needs a modifier, like *large* or *significant*.
plan ahead:	Eliminate *ahead;* all planning is ahead.
please be advised:	This sounds pompous; don't use it.
proved/proven:	Both are accepted; *proved* is more common.
revert back:	Eliminate *back*.
seem:	Try to avoid using this wishy-washy word.
take into consideration:	Say *consider* instead.
try to/try and:	Use *try to*.
unique:	Don't qualify this with *very* or *totally* (it means one of a kind, and it isn't comparable).

Words Most Commonly Misspelled

A
abbreviate
absence
abundance
accessible
accommodate
acknowledgment
advantageous
advice (noun)
advise (verb)
affidavit
allotment
allotted
all right
analogous
analyze
apologize
appearance
apropos
arrangement
assistance
assurance
attendance
authoritative
auxiliary

B
benefited
benevolent
best-seller
bookkeeper
bulletin
bureau
business

C
calendar
caliber
canceled

cancellation
catalog
catchword
censure
ceremony
changeable
characteristic
chargeable
chiefly
choose
chose (past tense)
clientele
column
commission
commitment
committed
committee
commodities
comparative
compelled
competence
competitive
complimentary
(no charge)
complimentary
(kind words)
concede
conceivable
conferred
confidential
conscientious
conscious
consensus
consul
convenience
co-op
cooperate
copyright
copywriter

corollary
correctable
correlation
council
counsel (advice)
counselor
counterfeit
courteous
courtesy
creditor
criticism
criticize
currency
customary

D
deceive
decision
deductible
defense
deferred
deficient
deficit
definite
definitely
dependent
desirable
devastate
development
diagramed
dictionary
difference
dilemma
diligent
disappearance
disastrous
discernible
discrepancy
diseases
dismissal
dissatisfied
dominant

E
earnest
echelon
eighth
eligible
embarrassment
emergency
eminent
employee
enclose
encouragement
enforceable
enlightenment
envelope
equally
equilibrium
equipped
equitable
equivalent
erroneous
essence
eventually
exaggerated
exceed
excellence
excerpt
exchangeable
excusable
exemption
exercise
exhaust
exhilarate
existence
exorbitant
extremely

F
facetious
familiar
fascinate
favorable
feasible

financial
flexible
fluorescent
focused
forcible
foreign
foreword
forfeit
formally
formerly
fortunate
fourth
frantically
frequently
fulfill
fundamental

G

gamut
gauge
generally
glamorous
glamour
glossary
government
grammar
grateful
grievance
guarantee
guidance

H

handicapped
handsome
harass
hazard
headache
height
helpful
hesitant
hindrance
homogeneous
humorous

hurriedly
hypothetical

I

idiosyncrasy
illegal
illegible
illicit
immaterial
immigrant
imminent
inaccessible
inaugurate
incidentally
incomparable
independent
inducement
inexhaustible
infinite
inherent
innocence
inoculate
inquiry
insignificant
installment
interfered
irresistible
itinerary

J

jealousy
jeopardize
judgment
judicial
juvenile

K

kernel
kidnaper
know-how
knowledge

L
labeled
laboratory
latter
legible
leisure
leveling
library
license
lightening
livelihood
loneliness
loose (adjective)
lose (verb)
lying

M
maintenance
manageable
mandatory
maneuver
meant
medal
medicine
medieval
mediocre
merchandise
miscellaneous
mischievous
misinterpreted
misspell
monotonous
morale
mortgage
municipal

N
naive
naturally
necessary
necessitate
negligible

neighbor
niece
nineteenth
ninety
noticeable
nucleus
numerous

O
obsolescence
obsolete
occur
occurred
occurrence
occurring
offered
often
omitted
opinion
ordinance (rule,
   decree)
originate
outrageous

P
paid
pamphlet
parallel
paralyze
paraphernalia
parliamentary
pastime
patience
peaceable
peculiar
perceive
performance
permanent
permissible
permitting
perseverance
persistence

personnel
pertinent
pessimistic
phenomenon
physical
plausible
pleasant
possession
practically
precedence
predominant
preferable
preference
preferred
prejudice
preparation
prerequisite
presence
prevalent
privilege
procedure
proceed
processor
proficient
profited
programmed
prominent
promissory
pronunciation
pseudonym
psychiatry
psychology
pursue

Q
qualitative
quantitative
quarantine
quarreled
questionnaire

queue
quiescent

R
racist
rapport
readily
readjustment
receipt
receivable
receive
recipe
recommend
recurrence
refer
reference
referred
regrettable
reimbursement
relief
relieve
reluctance
remember
remembrance
remittance
remunerate
rendezvous
repetition
resistance
restaurant
reversible
rhythm
roofs

S
sacrilegious
salable
schedule
scholastic
scrupulous
secretary

seize
separate
sergeant
serviceable
severely
shining
siege
significant
similar
simultaneous
statute
stereotype
studying
subsequent
subsidiary
subsistence
substantially
subtle
succeed
successful
succinct
superintendent
supersede
supervisory
supplementary
surprise
susceptible
sympathize
synonym

T
tactfulness
taxable
technician
tedious
temperament
temporarily
tendency
testimonies
thorough

through
tournament
tragedy
transfer
transferable
transferred
tremendous
truly
twelfth
tying
typical

U
ultimately
umbrella
unanimity
unbelievable
underrate
undoubtedly
unforeseen
unnecessary
until
usable
useful

V
vacancy
vacuum
vague
vehicle
vetoes
vice versa
vicious
vigilant
vigorous
vivacious
voluntary

W
waive
warranted

Wednesday
weigh
weird
wholly
witnessed

Y
yield

Z
zeros
zoology

AGREEMENT OF SUBJECT AND VERB

If	Then	Example
Names refer to books or magazines, or titles of articles . . .	they are considered singular.	*Consumer Guides* is published throughout the world.
Names of companies or institutions are considered a concept . . .	They are singular.	Sanders and Rosen, a successful accounting firm, was founded before I was born.
Are considered a plural subject . . .	they are plural.	Sanders and Rosen, certified public accountants, have prepared my tax returns.
Compound subject . . .	takes a plural verb.	The reaction and evaluation of each candidate have been assessed.
Compound subject joined by *or* or *nor* . . .	the verb agrees with the subject nearer to it.	Neither the ducks nor the duckling is eating the bread. Either the child or her parents are bringing the present.
Prepositional phrase separates subject from verb . . .	the verb still agrees with the subject.	One of his difficulties was his lack of attention.
Each, any, every, one, none, everyone, or *either* acts as subject . . .	the verb and accompanying pronoun are singular. (*None,* when construed as "not any," may be plural.)	Each of the women is planning her retirement. None of the boys is able to tie his own shoelaces. None of the employees are here.

If	Then	Example
Here or *there* begins sentence . . .	the subject usually follows and agrees with the predicate.	Here is the latest manual. There are the two books you wanted.
You use *as well as* . . .	the phrase doesn't affect plurality.	The manager, as well as the workers, feels sure the rule is unfair.
You refer to time, amounts, or numbers . . .	plurality depends on use.	Three days isn't enough time to complete the work. The $8,000 is to be repaid next year. These past four months have been rewarding.
You use *a number* . . .	it takes a plural verb.	A number of people are here.
You use *the number* . . .	use a singular verb.	The number of people present was small.

NUMBERS

If	Then	Example
One through ten . . .	spell out.	Only four children came.
Higher than ten . . .	use figures.	At least 14 students passed.
Mixed high and low . . .	be consistent.	I bought 4 rolls and 13 pieces of pie for the party.
Numbers beginning sentences . . .	spell out.	One hundred and six people attended.
Numbers representing numbers . . .	Use figures.	The vote was 7 to 4.
Units of measure or in sequence . . .		His score was 75. It measured 3 inches. Look for Figure 6 on page 22.
Ordinals: one or two words . . .	spell out.	This is the forty-second time I've tried it.
Longer than two words . . .	use figures.	This is our 103rd try this year.
Street names through tenth . . .	spell out.	She lives on Second Avenue. She lives at 210 East 42 Street.
Number for dates or streets . . .	don't use *th* or *st.*	June 21, *not* June 21st. East 75 Street, *not* 75th Street. *but* the 99th time.

USEFUL FACTS

U.S. Postal Service Abbreviations

Traditional and Two-Letter State and Territory Abbreviations

	Traditional Abbreviation	Postal Abbreviation
Alabama, State of	Ala.	AL
Alaska, State of	Alas.	AK
American Samoa	Amer. Samoa	AS
Arizona, State of	Ariz.	AZ
Arkansas, State of	Ark.	AR
California, State of	Calif.	CA
Canal Zone	C.Z.	CZ
Colorado, State of	Colo.	CO
Connecticut, State of	Conn.	CT
Delaware, State of	Del.	DE
District of Columbia	D.C.	DC
Florida, State of	Fla.	FL
Georgia, State of	Ga.	GA
Guam	Guam	GU
Hawaii, State of	Hawaii	HI
Idaho, State of	Ida.	ID
Illinois, State of	Ill.	IL
Indiana, State of	Ind.	IN
Iowa, State of	Iowa	IA
Kansas, State of	Kans.	KS
Kentucky, Commonwealth of	Ky.	KY
Louisiana, State of	La.	LA
Maine, State of	Maine	ME
Maryland, State of	Md.	MD
Massachusetts, Commonwealth of	Mass.	MA
Michigan, State of	Mich.	MI
Minnesota, State of	Minn.	MN
Mississippi, State of	Miss.	MS
Missouri, State of	Mo.	MO
Montana, State of	Mont.	MT
Nebraska, State of	Nebr.	NE
Nevada, State of	Nev.	NV
New Hampshire, State of	N.H.	NH
New Jersey, State of	N.J.	NJ

	Traditional Abbreviation	Postal Abbreviation
New Mexico, State of	N.M.	NM
New York, State of	N.Y.	NY
North Carolina, State of	N.C.	NC
North Dakota, State of	N.D.	ND
Northern Mariana Islands	No. Mariana Is.	CM
Ohio, State of	Ohio	OH
Oklahoma, State of	Okla.	OK
Oregon, State of	Oreg.	OR
Pennsylvania, Commonwealth of	Pa.	PA
Puerto Rico	P.R.	PR
Rhode Island and Providence Plantations, State of	R.I.	RI
South Carolina, State of	S.C.	SC
South Dakota, State of	S.D.	SD
Tennessee, State of	Tenn.	TN
Texas, State of	Tex.	TX
Trust Territory	Trust Terr.	TT
Utah, State of	Utah	UT
Vermont, State of	Vt.	VT
Virgin Islands	V.I.	VI
Virginia, Commonwealth of	Va.	VA
Washington, State of	Wash.	WA
West Virginia, State of	W.Va.	WV
Wisconsin, State of	Wis.	WI
Wyoming, State of	Wyo.	WY

Metric Equivalents

Linear Measure

1 centimeter = 0.3937 inch
1 inch = 2.54 centimeters
1 decimeter = 3.937 inches = 0.328 foot
1 foot = 3.048 decimeters
1 meter = 39.37 inches = 1.0936 yards

1 yard = 0.9144 meter
1 dekameter = 1.9884 rods
1 rod = 0.5029 dekameter
1 kilometer = 0.62137 mile
1 mile = 1.6093 kilometers

Square Measure

1 square centimeter = 0.1550 square inch

1 square yard = 0.8361 square meter

1 square inch = 6.452 square
centimeters
1 square decimeter = 0.1076
square foot
1 square foot = 9.2903 square
decimeter
1 square meter = 1.196 square
yards

1 acre = 160 square rods
1 square rod = 0.00625 acres
1 hectare = 2.47 acres
1 acre = 0.4047 hectare
1 square kilometer = 0.386 square
mile
1 square mile = 2.59 square
kilometers

Volume

1 cubic centimeter = 0.061
cubic inch
1 cubic inch = 16.39 cubic
centimeters
1 cubic decimeter = 0.0353 cubic
foot
1 cubic foot = 28.317 cubic yards
1 cubic yard = 0.7646 cubic meter
1 stere = 0.2759 cord
1 cord = 3.624 steres

1 liter = 0.908 quart dry = 1.0567
quarts liquid
1 quart dry = 1.101 liters
1 quart liquid = 0.9463 liter
1 dekaliter = 2.6417 gallons = 1.135
pecks
1 gallon = 0.3785 dekaliter
1 peck = 0.881 dekaliter
1 hectoliter = 2.8375 bushels
1 bushel = 0.3524 hectoliter

Weights

1 gram = 0.03527 ounce
1 ounce = 28.35 grams
1 kologram = 2.2046 pounds

1 pound = 0.4536 kilogram
1 metric ton = 0.98421 English ton
1 English ton = 1.016 metric ton

Approximate Metric Equivalents

1 decimeter = 4 inches
1 liter = 1.06 quarts liquid =
0.9 quarts dry
1 meter = 1.1 yards
1 kilometer = 0.625 mile

1 hectoliter = 2.625 bushels
1 hectare = 2.5 acres
1 kilogram = 2.20 pounds
1 stere or cubic meter = 0.25 cord
1 metric ton = 2,200 pounds

Index